Breaking the Silence:
From Shattered to Whole
A Story in Verse

Angela Mae Rivard

Potter's Wheel Publishing House
Minneapolis

Breaking the Silence: From Shattered to Whole
by Angela Mae Rivard

Published by POTTER'S WHEEL PUBLISHING HOUSE
MINNEAPOLIS
MN 55378

www.POTTERSWHEELPUBLISHING.com

© 2025 Angela Mae Rivard

All rights reserved. No part of this publication may be reproduced, stored in a retrieval system, or transmitted, in any form or in any means – by electronic, mechanical, photocopying, recording or otherwise – without prior written permission, except as permitted by U.S. copyright law.
For permissions contact:
info@POTTERSWHEELPUBLISHING.com

ISBN: 978-1-950399-25-3
LCCN: 2025940301

Table of Contents

Breaking The Chains

Happiness Isn't Meant For Me 1

Girl Behind The Scenes 2

Judging Eyes 3

Anxious Mind 5

Pain Within 6

Mirror, Mirror: Fractured Identity 7

The Demons Inside Of Me 9

Anxiety's Flame 10

Hide 12

Letter From Future Self 13

Reflections Of The Past 14

An Anxious Girl's Poem 16

Pain That I Deserved 17

The Life I Used To Want 18

Air 19

A Soul Adrift 20

Picture Perfect 22

Through Her Words 23

Beyond The Void 24

The Mind Is A Garden 26

My Worst Enemy 28

The Mask I Wear 30

Silent Screams 32

In The Dark Of The Night 35

Echoes In The Dark 37

The Weight Of Words 38

The Imperfect Repair 39

Nowhere To Run 42

Lying Awake 44

Bitter Taste 48

Monster In The Mirror 50

Confessions Of The Misunderstood 52

A Fragile Existence 54

Echoes In My Mind 55

I Am Darkness 57

Escuridão 59

Broken Pieces Of Me 63

Shadow To Bloom 65

A Warrior's Cry: Defeating The Demon Inside 67

Whispers From The Shadows 70

Wounds To Wisdom 72

The Demon's Grip 73

A Life With Anxiety 76

Embers Of Sorrow 79

Cheap Whiskey & Cigarettes 83

Dance Between Darkness And Light 84

Spell Of The Raven 86

Breaking The Walls

Salt On Skin 91

Keeper Of My Heart 93

He Saw Me 94

Through The Mud 95

I Miss You 97

Crash Into Me 99

Beautiful Oblivion 102

A Love Beyond Words 104

Fire In Your Eyes 106

Love's Thirst 107

Breaking Free

Tiny Flutters 113

Born Too Soon 114

Wrapped In His Love 115

Where Are The Stars? 116

Little One, I Prayed 118

Mommy, Are You Listening? 119

Operating Room Fears 120

32 Weeks, Part 1: Dad's Story 122

32 Weeks, Part 2: Mom's Story 125

32 Weeks, Part 3: Aiden's Story 128

The Journey Of Parenthood 131

Before You Were Born 133

Breaking The Silence

The Sun Shines Again 137

Free To Be Me 139

Work In Progress 140

A Shift In Perspective 141

Worthy 143

Exceptionally Me 145

Breaking Free	147
Shiny And New!	150
Authenticity Unveiled	151
Boundary Lines	152
Finding Peace In The Noise	154
Lead With Love	156
Invincible	158
Rising Above	160
Against All Odds	162
No Apologies	163
Whispers Of The Heart	164
I Matter, Too	165
The Light Within	167
My Own Story	168
Full Circle: My Writing Journey	169
Learning To Love Myself	171
Foreign	172
Inner Child	173
Ghosts	175
A New Dawn	176
Roots Of Resilience	177
Still Standing	180
Positive Vibrations	181
Real Beauty	183
The Lonely Heart (A 2-Part Poem)	186
Portrait Of A Poet	188
A Warrior's Scars: Journey To Inner Peace	190

Metamorphosis Complete!.. 193

Strength From The Struggle.. 195

The Raven's Wisdom 196

Shining Heroine.. 198

Forged From The Mud.. 201

Shadow To Flame.. 203

DEDICATION

*To my son, and to all who battle unseen storms.
May you always remember your voice is your strength, your scars are your stories, and you were never meant to suffer in silence*

FOREWORD
by Angela Mae Rivard

The first time I was bullied, I was in first grade.

I didn't understand why they called me "It" or a "Monster." I was the same as any other girl, just shy. What did I do to deserve being treated like this? I didn't understand why they laughed at me. I just remember the sting—the feeling that something was wrong with me. That moment was the beginning of a silence I carried for years.

The bullying followed me through school, wearing down my confidence, making me retreat further into myself. I stopped speaking up. I hid behind books, behind my bedroom door, behind a smile I hoped would keep people from asking too many questions.

My parents were kind and loving. But I never told them how bad it really was. I thought if I stayed quiet, I'd stay safe.

This book is my way of breaking that silence.

It's for anyone who has ever been made to feel small. For those who've buried their voice just to survive. These poems are pieces of my truth—my pain, my healing, and my power reclaimed.

I hope this collection reminds you that you're not alone. That your story matters. And that even in the quietest moments, your voice is still there—waiting for you to speak.

CONTENT WARNING

This book contains explicit depictions of mental illness, self-harm, suicidal ideation, trauma, and physical intimacy. It is intended for mature audiences. Reader discretion is advised.

Breaking the Chains

HAPPINESS ISN'T MEANT FOR ME

I am depressed. I will not be okay.

This is the way it must be. I must face the harsh reality.

Happiness walks past me, never making eye contact.

I press my face against the glass of joy, always outside.

Pain and misery cling to my soul, destroying what is left of me.

They have become my stronghold. The ones that love me try to uncover my pain.

They desperately try to make me feel sane, yet I still feel little to gain.

I try and try but it never lasts. My heart has been blackened with hate.

I reach for joy, but it vanishes like morning mist.

GIRL BEHIND THE SCENES

I'm known as the quiet girl, the girl who is always hiding behind the scenes.

I smile politely, but inside I'm breaking.

I perform with grace while my heart crumbles backstage.

My grin is a costume stitched over my shattered ribs.

I've always had so much to say. Too many times, I've let my demons get the best of me.

Every time I've tried to speak up, my demons told me to keep my mouth shut.

Now it's my time to shine, take center stage—dazzle in the lights like a queen.

I was scared and alone. Now I realize I don't have to fight this battle alone.

No more hiding. No more holding back. I am ready for the limelight at last.

JUDGING EYES

As I glance around, I sense the sting

of judging eyes, and the weight they bring.

A suffocating fog that clings and freezes,

filling my heart with pain, and my soul with pleas.

I wonder what they see, and whether they will know

the real me, beyond the surface level.

As I walk through crowded rooms, I feel the piercing gaze of judging eyes, like daggers that reveal

their darkness, their black and white views.

that don't see the full colors, the depth, the hues.

I hear the whispers, the criticism, the pain.

As people talk in hushed tones, watching me, judging my every step again.

Sometimes met with silence, stares that chill

laughing at my expense, with hearts of stone the sound echoing still.

But when you look at others, don't judge, instead,

gaze within, and discover the depths that lie ahead.

We must look beyond the surface level and discover the beauty that is concealed.

For only then can we truly love,

and create a world where hearts rise above.

Do not let judging eyes define

your self-worth, or your heart's design.

Instead, let love and kindness shine,

and guide you on your journey, one step at a time.

When you see someone, don't immediately judge,

look deeper, get to know them—

you might find they have a heart

that beats with kindness and love.

ANXIOUS MIND

Anxiety is deep within me. My thoughts spin like broken clock hands.

Each idea tangles like ivy choking a fence.

Intrusive thoughts are terrifying beasts that live in every corner of my head.

A storm raging, destroying everything in its path, leaving chaos and wreckage in its aftermath.

PAIN WITHIN

Young and reckless—blinded by your hollow smile. I stitched my trust into your shadow—what a costly weave.

You told me you care. I thought you would be there.

You left fingerprints of rejection across my skin. I limped from your love, wearing bruises where hope once lived.

The pain is embedded deep within—I can feel it crawling under my skin.

I try not to hold back or hesitate. The pain you left me is strong.

It's time to move on. I have carried the wounds from his gunshot for far too.

The echo rings beneath my ribs, too many nights I've bled that invisible bullet.

MIRROR, MIRROR: FRACTURED IDENTITY

Looking in the mirror, wishing I could change who stares back.

I get so sick of myself, the things that I lack. Inside, I feel broken and sad.

I fake a smile most days just to get through. I am running empty; I'm lost and confused.

Mirror, Mirror on the wall, I hate you because you tell the truth.

You remind me of all the mistakes I've made. All the burdens I carry and the prices I have paid.

Somedays my reflection winks with grace, other days it spits shards of shame.

The mirror sometimes offers kindness—other times it bares its teeth.

I don't want to see my reflection when it stares back. It reminds me of how lifeless I have become.

Only going through the motions because I always feel numb.

Mirror, Mirror on the wall, whisper the truth I've forgotten.

I don't know her at all. She turned into somebody different than she used to be.

My smile folds awkwardly, like paper creased in all the wrong places.

Even my smile seems borrowed like a mask never meant for me.

Now it's hard to fake a smile, I can only keep it up for a while.

Until the fake smile fades and I am left feeling incomplete.

The world sprints by, while I wade through molasses dreams.

While others leap ahead, I drag my breath behind me.

Mirror, Mirror on the wall, unravel the stranger staring back.

THE DEMONS INSIDE OF ME

I was once in a place so dark... I did not know my own heart.

I did not even know myself. Demons inside of me took over.

They crept—in shadows in my ribcage whispering lies in my lies.

Hushing me, in my sleep.

I was begging for help, but no one could hear me.

I gave in to the demons inside of me out of fear. I let them get in, take hold of me.

I turned into echoes of warnings I once gave others.

I once bloomed like spring—soft, kind and open. Now winter runs through my veins—sharp,

distant, frozen.

But there was still a fight inside me. I refused to be a quitter.

So, I fought my demons and pushed forward even on my darkest days.

Now, I stand in the light today. Light and free, I no longer will let my demons take hold of me.

ANXIETY'S FLAME

Fear's dark embers glow within,

the smoky air seeps down tightening my throat,

I can barely breathe,

let a word escape.

I feel the flames surge through my body,

sweat beads on my skin,

my face flushes red.

I clutch my chest,

gasping for air.

As I tumble into a pit carved by fear.

I smother it with silence, but it crackles back to life.

From a flicker to a flame, now untamed.

A whirlwind of emotions— caught in the crossfire,

a roaring inferno— consumed by the blaze.

Yet, in the ashes,

I find a spark, within my weary heart.

A flame of strength, a light in the dark.

I learn about meditation and mindfulness.

Slowly, inhaling exhaling, feeling each breath

I learn to calm the fire,

to find my voice, my heart's inner peace

and desire.

In a moment of stillness,

I hear my soul,

a whisper of truth,

that makes me whole.

I rise above with open palms, not to fight—but to cool the blaze.

It will be an ongoing battle, but I refuse to back down.

With hope and faith,

and every ounce of strength
   I have found in my darkest times,

My hope becomes drought—
   no fire left to feed.

Anxiety's grip will loosen
   its power over me,
      reduced to ashes.

HIDE

I want to disappear—fold into the wallpaper of this world.

Let me blend with shadows until I forget I exist.

I want to run away from it all, bury my head in my arms and cry.

I have been carrying the weight of the world for far too long. It is time for me to let it all go.

Release every emotion that I kept inside. I am tired of feeling broken.

become so numb from the pain inside. Sometimes, I just shut down.

I feel nothing at all, I want to forget this life. Let the pieces fall away.

It does not matter anymore. I do not care about anything.

No motivation. I have given up. I hurt so much.

Life carved its name into me with a jagged edge.

Each day it slices deeper where old wounds barely sealed.

It feels like everything crashes down on me. Suddenly, I could not breathe.

I'm crying, begging for someone to rescue me.

Rescue me before I hit rock bottom before it is too late before I fade away.

If you hear this silence, follow this trail to me.

Please trace my footprints in the dust before they vanish.

LETTER FROM FUTURE SELF

Scars trace her story like constellations of sorrow.

She just wants to be happy again—to stop feeling the pain that traps her inside.

She used to be happy, a free spirit. Somehow, she lost herself along the way.

When she was stumbling down the broken road, she felt like she was alone.

This is a letter from my future self, saying: *Hang on, beautiful girl.*

The dark clouds will pass. Someday, you will be happy again.

Your parents and siblings will be there for you, just like they always have.

You will meet your husband. You two will have a beautiful baby.

He will have your lips, your husband's nose. His eyes will be a mixture of both.

So, hang on, girl. It may be tough right now, but you'll get through.

You have God, friends, and family with you the whole time

Your future son will be waiting—you don't want to let him down.

Sincerely,

Your future self.

REFLECTIONS OF THE PAST

I once knew a girl who was so tired. Tired of being left behind and forgotten.

She was a misfit for most of her life. She wanted so badly to end her inner strife.

Before it was too late, she thought many times about ending her own life.

She wanted to call out for help but felt like nobody would hear.

Her soul stretched out like open hands, waiting to touch.

She wanted to let go of her fears.

But she was afraid to leap. It felt out of reach and far too steep.

Every night, she cried; she felt like she was drowning inside.

Drowning in her tears and sorrow.

I want to reach out to her now, tell her things will be better tomorrow.

Our time on this earth is short. Our time on this earth is borrowed. I still see this girl today, in fact, I see her every day.

Today, I look at her in a new way as I look in the mirror, and she stares back.

This time with a smile. She has come a long way to get rid of the pain she kept inside.

She realized letting go and letting God take control was her key to happiness and a better life.

Looking at her today reminds me of my former self.

What I have been through and where I am now.

As I look at her, I realize she will always be a part of me.

I've come a long way; she will always be part of me.

When I look at her, I will always see reflections of the past because that girl was...me.

AN ANXIOUS GIRL'S POEM

I am beautiful one day. Ugly the next.

I wish I could just get my life together. Gain some confidence. I am just one big mess.

Most days, I am ashamed of myself. I feel like I am fucking crazy and need some help.

I have anxiety over things that other people say mean nothing.

They say trivial and unimportant, but I cannot help what I worry about today.

I worry every day about everything, big and small.

Sometimes I feel so trapped that no one cares at all.

Suffocating myself, every day, most of the time, over things I cannot control.

Why am I such a freak? Why can't I just relax and breathe?

This is an anxious girl's poem.

PAIN THAT I DESERVED

I used to cut myself so I could feel pain.

Pain that I thought I deserved for all the problems in my life.

I felt like a no-good, nothing all the time. Like a girl who could never do anything right.

It was always my fault. No one knew except a few. I kept it a secret from everyone I knew.

Nobody ever really knew how close I was to coming completely unglued.

I thought about ending my own life many times.

If it were not for God, I would not be here today. Authoring this poem and spilling my guts for all to see,

It is all worth it if it helps just one person, one day.

I was able to get through that challenging time, and God was waiting for me on the other side.

I hope someone will read this one day, and their life will be changed.

Realize they are not alone and do not have to hide.

THE LIFE I USED TO WANT

She lives the life I used to want. She is beautiful and popular.

She has every guy in school chasing after her. Bowing down at her feet like she is the queen.

She has the cutest clothes. Her hair always looks neat. I have never seen her have a bad hair day.

For the 2nd year in a row, she was voted Homecoming Queen.

While girls like me are just trying so hard to fit in.

I blend into the background while she stands out in a crowd.

She dates the quarterback and has a flock of friends.

As I blend into the background, I realize I don't need her life to be happy.

I am happy to be me; I am blessed to have an amazing family and a few close friends.

That's all I need.

AIR

The room closes in; the air thins like trust.

The room is getting smaller, I swear. It is becoming too much to bear.

The walls are closing in; my heart is fluttering like a bird trapped in a cage

desperate to escape.

A suffocating fog, heavy with anxiety weighing down every breath.

I swear I'm not crazy. I just get anxious at times.

Someone, please help me. I need some air. Is anybody there?

Desolate and afraid. I clawed at the silence; lungs folded like paper.

Left to my own devices, I am a victim of my own vices.

A shattered mirror reflects back shards of my fragmented mind.

A SOUL ADRIFT

Silence pours sorrow into my soul, echoes rolling through a moonless night.

I search for a whisper in the dark, a glimmer of hope, in the abyss of the night.

I wander down a shadow-drenched street, where life, hopes, and dreams cease to exist.

I am shattered, lost in the fray. Bitterness is a wilderness of festering wounds

That reek of decay. Between the waves of despair and anxiety's disrepair,

My journey in life has gone astray. This is not the life that I dreamt,

The beautiful life I had conjured up in my head.

I saw the bigger picture; the beauty of what could have been…

only for it to fall flat and fade black. The ghosts of my past still linger,

Haunting me in my dreams. Shadows of regret chase my every step while I sleep.

I am left alone in this desolate landscape,

Searching for a glimpse of hope, a sign to hold on to, not to give up on myself.

I fear I am destined to roam this world forever lost, adrift without a cause, a purpose in life.

Drifting aimlessly through heavy clouds of doubt, burdened by doubt and shame.

But that is the price I paid for the choices that I made, a life of seclusion and disconnection.

But at least I am free from the weight of judgment.

That others push against my chest. Suffocating me, from within.

Lonely but free, I will wander into the moonless night, where the echoes roll into the light.

PICTURE PERFECT

She's a picture-perfect girl in a picture-perfect world, or so it seems.

Framed in expectations, posing through the ache.

She's beautiful and talented.

Her life looks like a fairytale from the outside.

If you dig a little deeper, you will see she isn't as put together as she seems.

She is falling apart at the seams, ready to break.

The stress of her life keeps piling up, she does not know how much more she can take.

A portrait with painted lips while fractures spider the frame.

Deep down, she is hanging on by a thread.

A melody stuck in a repetitive loop.

It is the alone time that she dreads the most.

She feels like a melody with discordant notes, out of tune.

That she never does anything right. They tell her, "You will better do next time."

If only she could see is worthy of her life and more—

and escape her inner strife before her demons bring her down one last time.

THROUGH HER WORDS

And she bleeds through her words. To show the pain she deserves.

She feels so empty inside. Her smile is a painted mask over hollow halls.

She has so much pain hidden behind her eyes.

Each word she pens, a flare shot into the night.

She is crying out for help. She is out of control and cannot save herself.

Somebody stops her before she falls apart.

Before she breaks down and becomes a danger to herself.

BEYOND THE VOID

Hopelessness echoes throughout the void; she is broken, lost.

Tries to reach out, but at what cost? Trapped in a desolate landscape,

she feels like no one is listening, more concerned with themselves—it is sickening.

She casts her voice into the abyss, unanswered

But once again her empty pleas get lost in the void.

She yearns for connection, but the more she screams out.

They say she is starving for attention.

Everyone does their best to avoid the sad, broken girl, while they go on with their lives in this chaotic world.

Time keeps ticking, the earth still spinning—she is stuck in a state of wishing.

Wishing her life were better, thinking she would be farther ahead by now,

she feels stuck in a state of limbo. Some days she wonders what it would feel like

to soar out of that open window, she always wanted to fly—it stays a freedom left untried.

I wish I could tell her: stay strong, it will be alright.

I am her inner voice, but she pushes me back down.

Inner phantoms roar, silencing my whisper.

She feels like her mind is under attack.

I believe if she holds on and listens to herself,

She will find the courage to heal one day, to release the pain behind her cry.

She just must take the first step forward and try,

Only then will she find there is more to life beyond the void.

THE MIND IS A GARDEN

A labyrinth of blooming ideas and thorny doubts,

often overshadowed by doubts and strife. In this inner sanctuary, roots grow deep.

Yet, fears and worries can make it hard to sleep.

In this garden of deep roots, complex thoughts and emotions bloom.

A haven for growth, where creativity flocks.

When anxiety's vines entangle choking growth.

Bringing to attention everything that I lack. This mental landscape, a field of dreams.

Where I can express myself and truly feel free. But even in freedom, there can be uncertainty.

The garden of my mind can become wild and carefree.

A vibrant tapestry, woven with lush greenery and flowers of every kind.

Even the most beautiful gardens can be fragile and hard to find.

For I am the gardener, the caretaker of my mind, I will cultivate beauty one thought at a time.

MY WORST ENEMY

A shadow that lingers, refusing to fade.

It slowly festers, becomes infected, and causes gangrene.

Depression seeps into my bones like a frigid winter chill.

A nasty, ugly beast that grips my soul.

It does not let go, sucking life and energy out of me.

Days blur as self-care withers away. The stench of despair clings to my filthy skin.

The darkness consumes every part of me, yet I feel numb, like emotions frozen in time.

When I look in the mirror, I do not recognize myself.

I see a distorted reflection, a funhouse mirror's lie.

I have turned into a lifeless person, barely human.

My shoulders slump, heavy with the weight of depression.

Each breath is a struggle, a physical force pressing down.

I go through the motions, feeling no excitement or joy.

I neglect loved ones, leaving messages unread.

The silence is deafening, a constant reminder of isolation.

Shadows creep across walls, darkness closing in.

Voices whisper in my mind, urging me to stay in bed.

I am living on the edge, any moment I could snap.

My appetite is gone; food tastes like ash.

My mind is a battleground, under constant attack.

Missiles and grenades fire off, throbbing headaches as the result.

On my worst days, I have contemplated a world without me.

But it's only been a fleeting thought; I push it aside.

Yet, I fear it may linger, a constant, haunting dread.

What would happen if I were gone? A thought too hard to bear.

Depression is my worst enemy; why must I face it alone?

The world moves on, smiling, while I struggle to atone.

Throughout my life, depression has come and gone.

But I won't give in. I will fight, though the battle's long.

I will rise above the darkness and shine, though my heart is wrong.

I may be battling depression, but I refuse to be defeated.

THE MASK I WEAR

A painted grin shields the ache within, fraying at the seams, a fragile disguise that has lost its dreams.

They see the smile, not the storm behind my teeth.

Now I must confront my deepest fears, shatter the illusions that bring me tears.

It is time to unmask, to let my true self shine, to emerge from the shadows and be divine.

I have been hiding behind my shield for too long,

I've been consumed with my faults and all that I do wrong.

Concealing my heart and silencing my song.

With every thread that is torn away, I feel the weight of fear and shame.

A new path unfolds, to a brighter day, where authenticity and hope proclaim.

I will rise; you will hear my name!

Now I will run forth unafraid, ready to exclaim everything I have held back.

My spirit is no longer under attack. As I step into the light, I am free to be,

My true self, wild and carefree.

No longer held back by fear and doubt, I rise and let my spirit soar.

SILENT SCREAMS

Do they hear my anguish, my desperate pleas? I feel like my voice is trapped, lost in the darkness.

Am I destined to live in the shadows, unseen? Alone in my room, I call out into the abyss,

the silence is deafening, a heavy stone that presses upon my chest.

I see my shadows dance upon the walls, the only thing that listens is my echo.

I try to use my voice, they miss the storm behind my smile, the flicker in my gaze.

What am I, invisible? My silent scream ricochets inside, echoing off ribcage walls.

The darkness closes in on me, suffocating me with its oppressive weight.

I am consumed by desperation, screaming silently for someone to acknowledge my existence.

Instead, they are consumed with their voices, a deafening noise that drowns out my cries.

I'm too young to be this broken. Will I ever grow up to find my token?

How will I know when my inner voice has spoken?

Too many questions for a girl my age. I am only twelve, at my awkward stage.

The smell of rain reminds me of better days,

but now it is just a distant memory, a fleeting glimpse of happiness.

My skin feels like it is crawling, and my heart is a heavy burden.

I am wrapped in a blanket of sadness, unable to escape.

Hold on, a minute—the phone is ringing... "Hello?" I answer, unsure who is on the line.

"It's your future self," the voice says.

"Don't worry, everything will work out. You'll learn and grow and find your way."

"What? I'm not allowed to talk to people I do not know. Is this some kind of joke?"

"But you do know me quite well, I'm in the future, letting you know to stay hold on, and stay strong."

"I don't know if I believe you..." "Believe it or not, I'm just stating the facts."

"Ok, well, thank you, bye." If what she said is true, I will find my voice, and it will shine through.

No longer trapped in the darkness and pain,

I will rise above, and my heart will regain its strength and courage.

I will break free from the shackles of my despair and use my voice to scream loud and clear.

I will be seen, I will be heard, I will be me, and my silent screams will finally be set free.

I will hold on to the hope that this might be true; it will be the guiding light that gets me through.

IN THE DARK OF THE NIGHT

In the dark of night, my shadows awaken. Like a murder of crows taking flight.

Their limbs stretch through the walls, and they speak in a haunting silence, whispering low.

Their voices echo through my mind, a cacophony of dread, a symphony of shadows.

A dance of despair, where lost dreams reign. With each fleeting heartbeat, they cradle my fears.

Night terrors woven from dread's silent thread.

Weavers of nightmare's silk, whispers in the devil's court.

The darkness is a heavy fog that clings to my skin, a cold, damp mist that seeps into my bones.

They taunt me with a cruel smile, "We are here for you, look closely, you can't escape now."

In this abyss where no light lingers, "we birth an existence beyond mortal chains."

Their voices like echoes ripple sharply through my mind,

a symphony that bends all my thoughts to their will.

"We dwell in the shadows, the depths of your soul."

Crushed by eternal darkness, my heart feels like lead.

"When you are at your weakest, we come to feed on our prey when our job is done, no light remains."

Together we linger in twilight's cruel grasp. I gasp for air until my inner demons are fed.

False friends, syrup-tongued, slither close and squeeze.

Promising in voices so sweet, "you will never be free, you will never be whole, we will devour your soul."

The wind whispers secrets in my ear, its breath cold and sweet, like a lover's kiss.

But the shadows are my true companions, my constant friends, my eternal foes.

There is no solace to be found when shadows exist.

They never stop; they always persist. In the murmuring of my heart, where no truth remains.

In this cage of darkness, a bird beats its wings. A desperate attempt to escape, but it is just a dream.

The shadows are the bars; the darkness is the lock. And I am the bird, forever trapped, never to rock.

Would fleeing this sorrow lead me to brighter days? Or will I forever be bound by chains?

Am I a lost soul now? A helpless bird forever trapped in a cage.

ECHOES IN THE DARK

Shudders in the darkness, lonely cries for help fall silent.

No one hears, no one comes. She is left alone, again, with only shadows.

Her heart knows the bitter truth: Nobody loves her; they just pretend.

Friendless, frozen, and forsaken, I crack under silence's weight.

No hand to hold, no soul to warm. But still, she holds on to a thread of hope,

a glimmer of light in the dark, an endless scope. A chance that someday, someone will hear,

and to warm her trembling silence through the cold. A whispered promise: she will rise.

In the darkness, a light begins to seep.

THE WEIGHT OF WORDS

Sticks and stones have never broken my bones, but their words have hurt me to the core.

Their cruel words stained my soul like ink-slow to fade.

They seeped into my heart, like poison in my veins, and echoed in my mind, with haunting memories that remain.

They made me question myself, my worth, and my name,

and left me feeling broken and forever changed. But still I rise, and still I stand,

and though their words still linger, I take back my hand.

I heal, I mend, I let go of the pain, and find my voice, to speak my truth, and break the chain.

THE IMPERFECT REPAIR

An arrow pierced my heart, and I stumbled backward, the scent of memories still lingers, a bittersweet reminder.

Fractured hopes and soul-crushing pain, every step forward feels like I'm walking, without purpose, without a name.

But I press on, determined to find my self again,

through the echoes of dark footsteps that I have been.

I had my life put back together, then it shattered like glass on the floor,

shards of my heart remain, as refracting light in fractured designs.

The pieces don't fit, the cracks show through,

a map of my pain, forever sewn.

As I navigate the darkness within, I'm learning to heal, these feelings I now deal

piecing together anguish that gnaws at my bones, with a persistent ache, I moan.

The art of healing, is an imperfect process,

one I'm slowly revealing, its hidden truths.

Mending a heart that's heavy and worn,

scars that linger, a mind torn with a topography of pain.

There's a loneliness in the steps I take,

cracked and empty, like the floorboards beneath my feet, they ache.

The sound that echoes from my hollow footsteps,

is of the heart's depletion, a sorrow that refuses to sleep. Instead its roots dig deep.

In the silence, I've come to realize, a lack of love causes internal bleeding, with a bitter taste that lingers. Shaded by an infidelity, where my heart and mind have cheated,

a conflict created, and loneliness has taken root, frozen, and immovable.

Over time, I've learned to rebuild,

finding my way back, out of the wreck.

As I reflect on the past, I realize,

I put up walls to shield myself from my pain, but loneliness crept in, and love remained as a stain ... my life in vain. Bittersweet memories linger,

promises shattered, a painful reminder of what could never be. Over time, I've learned to let go, focus on healing, and moving forward steady but slow.

Life is too short for anger and grudges on us to take hold, I've found peace in forgiveness, and a new path unfolds.

With each step forward, my heart becomes whole, the weight of regret slowly starts to fade, like morning mist that lifts, revealing warmth on my skin.

As I breathe in new hope, the scent of a fresh earth rises, to my senses surprise and I feel the gentle touch of healing's tenderness inside.

I've learned to weave the fragments of my soul into a new mosaic, my healing soul is made of this, one that shines with an imperfect beauty, mental health is now rooted in the reflection of my growth.

By Michael Lenhart & Angela Mae Rivard

NOWHERE TO RUN

Running as fast as I can, trying to escape. My self-destructive thoughts.

Trying to outrun. The incessant pain follows me every day.

I desperately need to get away. But where can I go?

Where can I escape? When there is nowhere to run.

Nowhere to hide. When all the pain is in my mind.

Every day, I feel so confined. The thoughts that haunt me are here to stay.

The reality is my pain will never leave. All I long for is inner peace.

I fear I will never know how that feels. I will never be able to live up to the world's ideals.

I have been running for so long, trying to escape.

But the pain is still inside me, like embers glowing in silence, hot but unseen.

I have tried to outrun the shadows, but they refuse to subside.

I have tried to silence the voices, but they are always whispering inside.

I will run through the city, through the night.

No matter how far I run, the pain will be my home.

It is a weight I carry, a burden I bear.

A reminder of past scars that will always be there.

So, will keep running through the joy and the pain, the tears and laughter,

through love and shame. I am fighting against my shadows that whisper my name.

But I will keep running until I find my way to a place where love will heal my heart and soul someday.

LYING AWAKE

Lying awake at night, thoughts race like startled deer in moonlight.

A million thoughts are rushing through my chaotic mind.

Replaying all the mistakes that I made in the past. I see my whole life in black and white

Like a movie that you cannot rewind. The tape of my life unravels before my eyes

I'm overthinking it all. What is next in line? Where to go from here now? I see no road signs

If only I could close my eyes, wake up fine, the next time,

that works most of the time, until I remember. The shambles my life has become.

I feel stuck every day, with nowhere to run.

I do not need saving; I don't want to hear any advice. I just want to be left to my own devices

I am not as happy as I seem. I have learned to fake a smile for the world

My two inner voices, darkness and light. Each is fighting for their turn in line.

Lying awake at night, overthinking everything. Closer to the brink, now everything is out of sync.

Now my life is at stake, all I want is a break without all these consuming thoughts taking over my brain

Insomnia, anxiety, depression, manic episodes. Are some of the things I have dealt with my whole life?

I am not all that crazy compared to some, but some days I feel like I am falling apart, bursting at the seams.

No one would lock me up in a padded room, if it came down to it, locked somewhere, key thrown away,

because sometimes I feel that is where I should be. It is hard to manage my mental instability

I do not want to spend my whole life taking pills. From a script that my doctor sent.

There must be more to this life than that. Hope I do not end up in a ditch somewhere, dead.

I must work twice as hard to live a more positive life. I had to teach myself to look at the bright side.

Lying awake at night, a chaotic mind, brain-dead. Confused about what is happening all around me.

The colors fade away; I see my life in black and white.

Day by day, like a movie that I watched multiple times.

Once I was up on cloud nine, now a stowaway.

The same old story unravels; It's Groundhog Day.

The clock's ticking, but time is running slow nowadays.

Feeling better does not feel better; it is now a daze.

This time it's me against myself; I have no counter plays.

I see my shadows everywhere; It's time for me to go away.

I always bring trouble to the table; I keep speaking irrationally.

From one person to another, I became partially.

Wish I had the power to pause all my problems for a day.

I have already paid the price for my sins; I am done with this layaway.

Need to break out of this loop and go somewhere peaceful, far away.

A friend of mine told me to grow through what you go through.

I take things one day at a time to see things through.

The sky's still blue, and I've got many dreams to pursue.

Lying awake at night, my mind is busy planning what lies ahead.

My thoughts are clear and focused; I'm going to aim at the head.

With a whirlwind of ideas and a memory like a steel trap, I tread.

I don't live in the past anymore; I look at what is at stake instead.

I am better at handling panic attacks now; I sort out the mishaps.

Many questions were thrown at me when I was looking for answers.

I can cut through the noise that surrounds me and focus on what matters.

Things go south sometimes, now I'm better at handling such patterns.

Not all dreams come true, but they are true. Still, my hope is not shattered.

I had a premonition that I was not destined to be a throwaway.

Not all broken things need fixing; that is my main takeaway.

We all are creatures of habit, from drugs, I slowly break away.

Feeling better does feel better now; depression does wear away.

Every day is a new chapter; in other words, it's a trick or treat.

I'm not afraid to make mistakes, but not all the mistakes I want to repeat.

My life will always be incomplete, but I see it as work in progress.

I do not crave what other people possess or what some others profess only believe in the process

I follow; I don't leave things undone midway. Rapture is on the way, and I am dressing up straightaway.

By Jordan Rains & Angela Rivard

BITTER TASTE

Memories of the past linger, a bitter taste that clings to my tongue.

Most of the time, I push the painful memories aside, yet my past always comes back to haunt me.

Like a ghost riding on my spine.

I know all too well the mistakes I've made, the immaturity I lacked.

I just want to move forward once and for all,

forget about that part of my past and every downfall.

I have lived and learned from every mistake, but still, every time I am reminded, I feel a sting.

I cling to my writing and the freedom it brings.

My fingers tremble with purpose every time I pick up my pen.

Writing helps me release all my feelings inside.

it has become a constant on which I can rely.

But writing is more than a coping mechanism.

it has been my anchor in turbulent times. If anyone ever tried to take it away,

I do not think I could survive. Even with writing, the demons of my past still torment my soul,

for the vulnerability I put into my writing is a trigger that I hold.

So, how do I confront the demons of my past and finally move on?

Well, do you think if I knew the answer, I would be writing this poem?

I just take it one day at a time. As time passes, I may begin to feel a glimpse of happiness that is real.

I will continue to rise, with hopes that with each step that I will heal.

MONSTER IN THE MIRROR

A reflection of pain, a childhood of shame. Low self-esteem, a heart that bore the blame.

Kids at school were cruel, their words like a knife; I was too shy to stand up—a silent, helpless life.

I was an easy target, or so they'd claim, but their words cut deep, leaving scars that remain.

I would cry myself to sleep, feeling worthless and alone.

A morbid thought would creep in: *"Maybe I'd be better off gone."*

Their voices razors dressed as laughter, tore at my becoming.

Their harsh words echoed—a constant, haunting creed.

Invisible and numb, I felt like a ghost in the hall.

A nickname—"monster"—stuck, a painful reminder of it all.

But I rose above, I found my voice, I stood tall.

I forgave those who hurt me and began to heal from it all.

I'm a mom now strong and confident, a survivor of the pain.

I will teach my son to stand up for himself, to never inflict hurt in vain.

To those who bullied me, I say: "I forgive, I'm free."

You *helped shape me into the strong woman I am meant to be.*

I hope you've learned and grown, so that you will teach your kids to be kind.

Let us break the cycle of bullying, let love and empathy shine.

If my story helps just one person, then I have done my part.

Let's stand together against bullying and create a loving heart.

CONFESSIONS OF THE MISUNDERSTOOD

It's not fair that some people live their whole lives misunderstood—

Never able to live up to the expectations that others hold them to.

They march in a rhythm only their hearts can hear. They may not follow all the rules you abide by.

They have good hearts. All they want is to be loved for who they are.

These are the confessions of the misunderstood.

The rejects, the unloved, the ones who may be too afraid to speak up.

When someone doesn't quite get who they are, they see a strange behavior or quirk—

they automatically turn away, how is that fair!?

The world is missing out on so many great people just because they act a certain way.

These are the confessions of the misunderstood: the ones who got bullied in school,

the misfits, the geeks, the losers, the girl who was just too shy.

They liked to throw out labels, make fun, to make themselves feel better, but everyone knows now:

bullies are deeply insecure. It is okay, *we see you now*:

You are loved, you are seen, you are understood.

To all broken, the hurt, and the lost: I want you to know—you are not alone.

I'll be your friend when you need Someone to turn to.

These are the confessions of the misunderstood.

We are more resilient than we are ever given credit for.

We will rise from the ashes.

Stand together, arm in arm. Sing a song of hope.

A FRAGILE EXISTENCE

Don't be alarmed by my darkness,

It's only my conscious talking, letting her suppressed feelings out.

I have been trapped in the walls of my mind.

A bird with tattered wings, clawing at a cage carved of its own breath.

I search for a key to unlock my chains. But find myself lost in my refrain.

Mental anguish, whispered screams in the back of my mind,

The weight of my thoughts, a burden left behind

Don't be startled by my melancholy, a sorrow that clings to every part,

feelings of bitterness seeping into my heart.

I lead a fragile existence, forever worn, where darkness whispers, I am known.

Don't be alarmed, though I'm consumed.

ECHOES IN MY MIND

Walking empty city streets, early morning's chill, cars hum around me, exhaust fumes' bitter fill.

Fresh rain's scent rises, a fleeting calm descends, but then, the whispers start, an eeriness that never ends.

I hear a cacophony of faint whispers in the distance,

as I walk closer, they grow increasingly louder, and I admire their persistence.

Now the voices are loud, they are borderline shouting, and my ears are pounding.

But yet, I still can't make out what they are saying. Are these people crazy?

I see an outline of figures, dark shadows, from afar.

Blurred outlines hover, identities cloaked in fog.

Finally, I reach them, I stand where they were, but there is no one there.

This doesn't make sense; they were just here...

Let me think for a second, how could this be?

What is it that chased me? Shadows, ghosts,

Do they come to visit me? Or a frightening hallucination, a loss of sanity?

I hear the gentle hum of self-doubt like a bee buzzing in my ear, a never-ending, high-pitched itch, I cannot escape it.

I am struck with fear; anxiety overwhelms me like a dark cloud of an approaching storm.

My shadows carry names I've never dared to ask.

I AM DARKNESS

I am darkness. Darkness is me.

No one wants to talk about the darkness. I feel it come over me.

Like a soft blanket of snow that covers a winter night.

I feel the darkness come over me and grab me tight.

First, it is lovely and inviting. Sexy and enticing. It lures me in.

Captures me and sucks me in. Its menacing claws grab hold of me.

Put me in a choke hold. The pressure on my throat is too much to bear.

I try to break away, but the darkness threatens, "Don't you dare." I am darkness. Darkness is me.

The darkness has become a part of me. Hardening my soft heart all my life.

Clouding my vision and adding strife. If only I could escape. But I do not see a way.

If I let the darkness go, I know I will miss it so...

I am darkness. Darkness is me.

Do not be fooled by my smile, it is all just a ruse. To leave everyone confused.

I am a goth queen. The darkness has slithered its way deep into my soul.

My inner being. There is now darkness behind every feeling.

I am darkness. Darkness is me. That is the way it will always be.

I cannot fight the darkness so; I welcome it in like my closest friend.

I am darkness. Darkness is me.

I will no longer pretend to be something I am not.

When I know I am a child of darkness. A wicked little bitch.

Satan does not scare me.

I dined with demons, their breath warm with lies I once swallowed.

I have disturbing conversations with my dark self.

If I repeated it out loud, people would say I need help.

My sanity unravels like thread in the wind.

I am a certified lunatic that creeps in the night.

Darkness and I have learned to coexist. We started a secret love affair, a tryst.

Darkness has made me strong and powerful. Gave me an iron fist.

I am darkness. Darkness is me.

ESCURIDÃO

Darkness, Absence of Light.

Starting every day with a smile is a lot harder than it sounds.

I ask myself most days, am I really living? Or do I just exist?

I often have thoughts that tell me I'm not good enough.

No matter how hard I try to escape these thoughts...they will not quit.

Deep down, I know I am better than the dark thoughts that invade my mind.

So, why do I get so concerned about my flaws and the things that I lack?

I try to be happy but the dark side of me keeps showing its ugly self.

Looking at me, most people would never know I have a long history or self-sabotage and abuse.

My whole life I have been numb and confused.

It's about time I wake up and tell my demons to shut up.

I used to have thoughts of self-harm.

I felt like I would get a little relief if I just cut my own arm.

I deserved it...for the pain I caused.

Without darkness inside of me, I feel like I am lost.

I want to be happy. I really do.

But my pain manifests itself into a place so empty.

I am too numb now to navigate my way out.

You see, darkness and I are attached at the hip.

It clings to me, and I cling back.

Darkness drips like morphine-familiar, fatal, and sweet.

Happiness for me is a long and winding road I am still traveling through.

I could ask somebody for a road map but what good would that do?

No one understands my pain. They cannot see that I am broken from the inside out.

That there is a real sadness in my pout. I often wear a fake smile on my face.

I feel like I must stay in hiding. I have tried to be happy, but my fears are abiding.

No one wants to deal with a soul as dark as mine.

My heart is a vault, keys lost to time.

If I let you get close, you are one of the few.

Like flies on a carcass, dark thoughts swarm through my head.

Some days I have thought, I would be better off dead.

Happiness is a feeling I have only experienced for short periods of time.

I wonder if one day if I will find true happiness that is mine.

Would I know the feeling of happiness though if it came knocking on my door?

When I come face to face with real happiness.

I hope it is not something I ignore.

I want to stand tall and choose to be happy.

Despite my mistakes and downfalls.

That is something I am still learning how to do.

Some days I feel like a baby still learning how to crawl.

I told the dark side of me to leave long ago. Yet, it hangs on to what is left of me.

It won't get a clue. I'm still holding on too tight. I need to try harder if I ever want to see the light.

I like to remain mysterious and perplexing. Hide myself from others.

Keep them guessing. Like a sleuth. My mental illness makes me stagger and afraid to talk to strangers.

People tell me I am strange. They do not get that poets are prone to things like depression and anxiety.

That there is a cost for creativity. Some people have called me bi-polar.

Others call me insane. Unless you are a doctor. Please, do not diagnose me. I have tried it all.

Pills and therapy. Self-help books, meditation, and prayer. I still have not found the answer.

Sometimes I swear I am getting crazier as the days go by.

Other times I am fine. I will not give up. It may be a long journey to be happy.

But I know it will be worth the wait. Besides, I don't know how much more darkness I can take.

Darkness is the absence of light. But for me, it is also a condition.

I am tired of being in a constant downward state and reliving all my mistakes.

I deserve to be happy after all I have been through.

Happiness does not come easy for me. I doubt it ever will.

It's something I must work on. To strive for all the time.

I grow tired of telling people I am fine. I want to choose to be happy even on the bad days.

To wear a smile that is not fake. To distance myself from anger and hate.

I refuse to wallow in my own self-pity.

I am living in depression town but I long to visit the happy and bustling city.

It is a process that is difficult. I sometimes wonder if I will make it out okay on the other end.

But on the flip side of darkness. Happiness is still waiting for me. Accepting the invitation is all up to me.

BROKEN PIECES OF ME

Shards of glitter on the floor of silence, exposed and raw, laid out for all to see.

For too long I have tried to hide from pain, from everyone, including myself, in vain.

I will no longer hide any part of me. From joy to fear, I will lean into vulnerability.

Let it sink in, so I can finally be myself again, wild and carefree.

The moments, the life I've been waiting for, can finally begin, like an open door.

I have stopped hiding, become more confident, I have learned to let others back in, persistent.

My heart was buried under mounds of hurt, from everything I have been through, I have been torn.

I held so much pain inside, it is true, I just kept kicking dirt, instead of seeing it through.

Maybe I was lost or just so afraid, to face the hard truths, the ones that I have made.

But today I stand tall, over the ground, that held me down, with a heart that's unbound.

These are the broken pieces of me, Raw and exposed, laid out for all to see.

I am not perfect, never claimed to be, just a soul, healing, spiritually.

These are the broken parts of me, accept me or not, it is all the same to me.

I no longer need validation from others, like I used to, so badly, in desperate covers.

These are the broken parts of me, picked up and put together again, I am free.

I am stronger than I have ever been, a phoenix rising from the ashes within.

SHADOW TO BLOOM

If gaze into the abyss, where only shadows exist.

Will I be able to resist? I dangle in the dusk half-submerged in silence.

But here's the twist: what if I am but a shadow lingering through this life,

a lost and lonely soul, roaming the world alone?

Now, everything makes sense. All my life, I have felt like I have been drifting away…

Ideation of darkness and death… disassociated to the core.

Yet, I have always wanted more. The question is, where do I go from here?

If I were offered a chance to live, putting my shadow self behind,

would I take it? Or would I sink further into the abyss?

As I walk through the abyss, icy winds

hit my face, the smell of smoke is in the air, the abyss mirrors my soul, a void of disconnection.

Trapped in the darkness. I see a faint light at the end, but I am scared.

Perhaps, in this light, I will find my chance to thrive,

to leave the shadows behind and start anew Rae.

A glimmer of self-awareness sparks within as I take my first steps towards the light.

As I approach the end of the abyss, near the light, a lotus flower pulses through the soot—its petals daring to blink, its petals slowly unfurled.

My heart softens, and I realize I am the flower, with roots buried deep, yet blooming, reaching for the sun.

In this moment, I am transformed, reborn, my shadow self-released, as I emerge into the light.

With one breath, I let go of the darkness and step into the radiance, ready to live.

A WARRIOR'S CRY: DEFEATING THE DEMON INSIDE

In the depths of my soul, a demon resides.

A constant companion, born with my first cries.

With eyes that glow like embers, he watches me roam.

I am a lone wolf, wandering, forever lost, forever home.

His voice—a storm breaking inside me, makes my soul crawl.

His body, a canvas of scars and pain etched into his flesh, like a twisted, cruel refrain.

His face, a map of anger and disdain, a heavy, scowling expression, was forever etched in his brain.

His eyes glow with a fierce intent as if daring the world to cross him, to tempt his wrath and bend.

He feeds on my fear, on my doubts, and my shame growing stronger with each passing day, his presence a haunting claim.

To the darkest corners of my mind, where shadows roam and play.

He lurks, a sinister figure, waiting to pounce and slay.

Joy was my birthright—until night swallowed the sun.

The bullies and my demon started to control my mind.

I became shy and isolated from my classmates, lingering in the halls alone, clutching my books.

In the hollow halls of my school, empty lockers stood down long, crowded hallways.

Faded posters whispered tales of their abandonment.

Harsh fluorescent lights flickered above, casting eerie shadows on deserted corridors.

Echoing footsteps, a solitary sound, reminded me I was alone.

Muffled laughs and whispers, a reminder of connections I couldn't make.

A constant reminder of my isolation, but in the darkness, a spark within me flickered to life, I was ready to end my inner strife.

I realized I was the one holding my lifeline, the one who could set myself free.

I am an angel, a warrior ready to battle until the war is won.

Reaching out, I found the strength to rise above

to shatter the silence, to speak my truth.

The sensation of my mouth zipped shut was painful, leaving my lips bloody and swollen, the pain inside, a gnawing ache.

Worse than any physical scar, too many times

I have been abandoned, ghosted, by those I thought were my pack, my friends.

But I have discovered that I am more than my scars, more than my pain, I am a survivor, a warrior.

I have been bullied, left alone, a wounded wolf abandoned by its pack.

But I have found my voice, my strength, my inner truth.

I will use my story to empower, to shine a light on troubled youth.

I will stand with others who have been broken and help them find their way.

Together we will rise, our voices loud, our spirits unbroken.

We will stand tall, we will shine our light, we will never be silenced again.

We will find solace in our voice, our strength.

We will learn to love ourselves, to heal, to mend, to rise above the pain.

WHISPERS FROM THE SHADOWS

I trailed the echoes of shadows into the darkness, the cave of the abyss, where no light dares to dwell.

I heard stories, tall tales, that those who travel down this path never make it back.

But I felt no fear, instead, I heard the shadows' despair.

Their wails clawed at the silence, yearning for escape.

I sensed the depth of their pain deep within my soul.

I yearned to free them from the turmoil they had seen.

The cries grew stronger, their shadows longer, revealing the shape of their hearts on the walls, as I walked further down.

Their eerie cries echoed within me, a haunting melody that I could not shake, I resonated with their pain.

My own heart ached with their agony, a symphony of sorrow,

a longing for a brighter tomorrow that I could not contain.

In their darkness, I saw a reflection of my own, a mirror held up to my soul.

From their torment, a fragile beauty bloomed reflecting my own awakening.

I realized their pain was not in vain but a catalyst for new beginnings and transformation.

Their emotions, like the human condition,

The shadows longed for connection, to be loved, to be understood…

Deep in the abyss, I listened to the shadows, their stories, their pain.

I discovered a strange sort of peace, a sense of solidarity,

as the shadows whispered their secrets to me.

I confronted my deepest fears,

I helped the shadows let go of the suffering they had held on to for so many years.

When I left the abyss, I felt a sense of newfound compassion and empathy.

And I knew as I walked out, the shadows and I were both free.

WOUNDS TO WISDOM

Licking the pain from old wounds, I have become consumed.

I reopened a door to the past, a thought shut long ago.

Life's first found me often—each blow a cruel sculptor's chisel.

A pathetic sight, wallowing in self-pity, trapped in misery.

If I seem desperate for attention, it's because I am.

I need someone to see me, truly me.

The girl I was before I was broken still lingers,

Buried deep, waiting to be unearthed.

I was stuck between memories that once seemed lasting.

Memories haunt me, but I will find my way to the light.

I have transformed, evolved—same heart, wiser, stronger.

I distilled pain into ink, wrote my way out of silence.

From scars, I stitched armor. From the ache, I built a voice.

THE DEMON'S GRIP

All my life, since I was a child,

a demon has lurked within me,

longing to be fed,

whispering uncertainty into my head.

Planting rotten seeds of panic and dread,

I am not sure how he came into existence,

but he gets angry when I am happy,

no matter how hard I try, I cannot seem to escape his wrath.

I desperately pray for a lighter path,

but he rears his ugly face.

Filling my mind with unpleasant thoughts,

I wish I could erase.

Instead, I find myself lost in a lonely haze,

Feeling uneasy, restless,

when my demon comes out,

It's hard to sit still, I just want to run away or shout.

When the demon arises, I see visions of red,

a fiery glow that spreads.

He preys on any inch of hope I have left.

I see his face, haunting me in my dreams.

Nightmares so frightening they make me scream.

I hear his voice whisper to me at night,

deep and raspy, a sound that sends shivers down my spine.

My heart races fast, my stomach out of whack.

My muscles tense up, my jaw clenches tight,

uncomfortable pulses run through my body,

leaving me drained and weak.

I tell people I am fine, but truth is I feel confined within the walls of my own mind.

A relentless critic, spreading fuel on my doubts and shame,

he points his gangly fingers at me, saying I am the one to blame.

He preys on my weaknesses on my weaknesses, when I am vulnerable, and scared.

I try my hardest not to listen,

yet, I cannot escape, I am trapped by the din, that lies within.

A cacophony of self-doubt and fear,

that brings me to tears.

The demon is a force, a controlling facade that will not let go

Clinging to my soul, leaving me feeling bitter and alone.

Will I ever escape his deranged hold, he has over my soul?

Or will I one day heal and be able to let go?

The noose around my neck, a constant weight,

too uncomfortable to bear.

I hope one day he tightens his grip,

that I can let go of his dark spirit.

I search for solace, in the midst of the darkness,

seeking refuge from his grasp.

I yearn for freedom from his hold,

a life untethered by his dark influence on my soul.

A LIFE WITH ANXIETY

Every day is a battle when you are fighting against yourself.

I have an inner struggle deep inside but hide it well.

I bury it so deep, no one can tell.

I am in a brawl with my demons all the time.

Shadows that haunt my thoughts, turmoil that entangles my mind.

No matter how hard I try I can't escape.

I feel trapped. I feel alone. I feel like nobody can hear my screams.

Too often I get lost in vanishing hopes and unreachable dreams.

Tantalizingly close yet slipping away, I can't seem to grasp happiness before it drifts away.

Happiness likes to tease.

I try my best to live freely and be happy.

Anxiety and depression take over every time.

My mind is never pleased.

I can never fully be at ease.

My brain is self-destructive.

Always beating itself up.

I just want to tell it to shut up.

I wish there was a switch to turn off the anxiety in my mind.

If only shutting off my anxiety was as simple as hitting a light switch.

Life would be much easier.

But we can't all get what we wish for.

I accept my anxiety as part of me,

I manage it every day.

There are days where I really struggle,

others where I am fine.

Maybe, it will get easier with time.

Sometimes I tell myself anxiety is the price I must pay for all the mistakes I have made.

I know that isn't true though,

the thought fades.

But my anxiety remains, locked in place.

Anxiety is like having a voice in the back of your mind that fills you with constant worry and self-doubt.

I get so frustrated I don't know if I want to cry or shout.

Sometimes I do both.

I vent to others and let it all out.

But I don't feel like they truly understand unless they have experienced mental illness themselves.

Anxiety is an illness.

But it's not like the cold or flu.

Medication can help but it will never fully go away.

I don't want to be dependent on pills.

My whole life I have tried to handle my anxiety and depression myself.

I search for peace but it's out of reach, a fleeting dream.

A life with anxiety will it forever be a constant theme.

Or will I find hope, learn to cope, realize that I don't have to fight this alone?

EMBERS OF SORROW

A mother's love is a flame that burns bright,

guiding her through life's darkest, most endless night.

In my enchanted kingdom, where ancient stones whisper secrets to the wind,

a mighty dragon lies, with a sorrowful call, her heart and soul entwined.

Her scales glimmer like moonlit opals, shimmering with a soft, ethereal glow,

as she protects her people, through the dark of endless night's shadowy, mystical woe.

The loud noises of the magical creatures fill the kingdom's air,

the chatter of pixies, the roar of unicorns, the laughter of centaurs without care.

Yet, the dragon pays no mind, lost in her sorrowful refrain,

her heart feels like a heavy stone, weighing her down with every beat, every pain.

The dragon's emotions rage like a thunderstorm,

rain pouring down, her tears, thunder and lightning, her anger's form.

Dark clouds gather, her sadness, a heavy heart,

yet, she wants to honor her child's memory, never to depart.

Turmoil brewing inside, a heart torn,

grief's dark clouds gather, and sorrow's lightning scars are born.

Yet, even in turmoil, a glimmer of hope appears,

a chance for healing, a new scope, through all her sorrowful years.

With fierce devotion, she defends this land,

for her child, she holds on to the past,

cherishing memories that forever will last.

She cherishes the memories of her child, before he was taken away,

killed by the castle's enemy army, in a brutal, senseless slay.

For hell is no match for the fury of a dragon mother scorned,

her wrath, a burning fire, that will never be torn.

Now enemy lines pay the price, for taking an innocent life.

As she gazes at the stars on a clear, midnight sky,

she's reminded of her child, his smile, his innocence, his enduring might.

She recalls the days she never let him out of her sight,

watching over him, with a mother's loving light.

But even in sorrow, there is a glimmer of hope,

a chance for healing, a new scope.

I, the princess of this fair land, sense

my dragon's pain,

and take her to a secret place, where love and magic reign.

The secret garden's sweet perfume, a gentle breeze that soothes her soul,

brings back memories of joyful times, and moments she desperately tries to hold.

She cherishes the memories of roaming free,

in fields of green, with her child, wild and carefree.

Lying next to him at night, keeping him safe,

as the stars shine bright with pride, and the moon's soft light illuminates their escape.

With every breath, she feels the ache,

of losing her child, her heart's mistake.

Yet, with time, she starts to interact,

With other dragons, and finds hope renewed.

A future where her heart can heal,

and love can bloom, and her spirit, too.

For her child, she stands loyal, to the kingdom, the princess, and the knights,

who watch over her, with honor and might.

Though sorrow's scar will forever remain,

her heart, a flame, burns, and loves again.

In sorrow's dark and endless night,

she finds the strength to carry on, a guiding light.

For in her kingdom, where shadows fall,

she guards her people, standing tall.

She rises, a phoenix, from the ashes cold,

her spirit unbroken, her heart, a flame to hold.

For she is a dragon, a guardian true and bold,

and her love and courage forever will be told.

CHEAP WHISKEY & CIGARETTES

There are memories from childhood we want to hold on to forever.

Others we wish could be erased like the stench of cheap whiskey and cigarettes.

This was my best friend's stepdad's signature taste.

His breath reeked of it, lingering as he forced his tongue down my throat.

I was fifteen, innocent and frozen in a nightmare that still haunts me like a shroud.

His stubble felt like sandpaper on my skin, a sensation that still brings memories of every unwanted touch.

Even now, my husband's prickly stubble takes me back to that place.

I was a good Christian girl, afraid to confess, afraid to speak.

But the truth was, I had done nothing wrong.

I was groomed, manipulated, and abused.

There are memories from childhood we want to hold on to forever.

This one I wish I could erase.

DANCE BETWEEN DARKNESS AND LIGHT

I was a shy and broken girl,

lost in the wilderness of life,

isolated, alone.

Then I heard a voice whisper,

"Never fear, there is hope."

Yet, along the way, I discovered my duality—

a dance between darkness and light.

In my darkest times, hope was my guiding light,

the only thing that kept me going through the night.

Though my journey was rough,

painful, and devastating at times,

I learned valuable lessons along the way.

I clung to hope, a beacon in the darkness,

and slowly, light began to seep through.

For so long, I submitted to society,

gave in to life's demands,

until I realized this is my life—

why am I letting others manipulate,

make decisions?

That little girl grew into a woman,

vibrant, loving, and full of joy.

She no longer walks through the wilderness alone,

but has a tribe, family, and friends by her side.

For they know her true heart,

the woman she is inside.

Though beautifully broken, I am now unapologetically free.

I started to listen to my heart's gentle call,

no longer quiet or meek,

I found my voice; I started to rise.

SPELL OF THE RAVEN

The power of the raven resides in the depths of my soul,

stirring inner pain and turmoil.

Between light and darkness, I dance

a delicate balance, a fragile secret in the palm of my hands.

The foggy gray eyes of the raven cast

an eerie spell,

one that draws me deeper into the shadows

With every breath, the raven's power grows, unstoppable,

a force that consumes me whole.

The darkness stirs, like a cauldron boiling from my soul.

As the cauldron boils, my grip on reality unwinds.

Bubbling with intrusive thoughts that refuse to sleep.

A lingering presence starts to creep.

The power of the raven brings a mystical energy,

an aura of darkness, where the madness within myself thrives.

The raven whispers secrets—too disturbing to children's ears.

In the raven's shadow, I confront the demons of my past,

the darkness whispers truths that will forever last.

Haunting images swirl through my mind.

The raven's cruel intentions never left behind.

I lost my grip; the raven's spell cast doom across my life.

In the darkest depths of my soul, I am yearning for the light.
Remnants of fractured memories, slipping through the cracks.
I walk among the skeletons of my past.

Breaking the Walls

SALT ON SKIN

Salt on skin, quite the sensation, I can taste the sweat, as our bodies get heated, your lips

Whispers of silk against my hunger. Featherlight kisses, drifting like falling petals.

I am yours tonight, wild and free. Tonight, I unravel into you untamed and free.

Your broad shoulders and strong arms make me safe and secure.

As your arms wrap around me, and you trace your fingertips on my unclothed body, you hold me closer.

Your warmth sparks lightning beneath my ribs. Electric currents rise where your skin meets mine.

Your warmth sparks lightning beneath my ribs. Electric currents rise where your skin meets mine.

Being intimate in the dark, our hearts beat together as one.

We give in to love's release, then we collapse, in each other's arms.

We will wake up with the sun, surrender to desire, once more.

For in each other's arms, we find our fun. In the heat of the moment and in the calm that follows, we know our love has conquered all.

We lose ourselves unbound and free. All barriers fall, we meet as fire meets air, a true connection of physical intimacy.

Each kiss etches eternity on my skin. In whispered oath, time bends around us.

KEEPER OF MY HEART

My heart rests in your careful hands—you guard my soul like a sacred flame.

With every beat, I feel you close. Each thump echoes your name.

You pulse through me, a rhythm all your own.

You understand me in ways I can't explain.

You read my silences like scripture. You speak the language of pauses.

Your love gives me strength.

Your love is the scaffold I rebuild myself upon.

In your love, I gather courage to be whole.

With every breath I melt into your arms and collapse.

Your love is a lantern guiding me in the darkest night, I'm a damsel in distress in a tower all alone,

You are my savior, my knight in shining armor—the keeper of my heart.

HE SAW ME

We are a cosmic connection written in the stars.

He read the footnotes I kept hidden in silence.

He held my broken pieces as if they were stardust.

When I couldn't meet my reflection, he met it for me.

He traced love into the silence between my words.

The way he noticed everything about me, things that others didn't see.

He saw me for me. I didn't have to pretend to be something I was not.

The first time I met him, he saw me, and that is something I will never forget.

He mirrored love in quiet gestures I almost missed.

I became a shadow in his footsteps; He showed me what love truly is.

THROUGH THE MUD

I crawled through grit, roots clinging to my ankles.

With every step I sank deeper, but when I saw your face, things became clearer.

In the mess of my journey, you were my solid ground.

When the storm was setting in, you were my guiding light.

You shone like the brightest star in the night.

Through the darkness and the grime, you were the love that carried me through.

Thorns tore at my spirit, but I pressed on.

You are my anchor in the sea; without you I do not know where I would be.

With you, I find the courage to face the darkest night.

Trudging through the mud with you, I find my strength.

Together we trudge through the mud, side by side.

Lifting each other, our bond is my greatest pride.

And with you by my side, I'm no longer stuck in the mud, I am turning it around

As I clean the dirt off my soiled feet,

I know you will always be there, because you have seen me at my worst, dirty and unclean.

And yet, you still choose to stay, and in your love, I am made clean.

Now I stand before you, washed and renewed,

you picked me back up, helped me bloom.

I am forever grateful for your love that saw me through.

The mud may still be there, but it no longer defines.

For with you, my love, I have found a love that withstands all.

Hand in hand, we will walk into the sunrise, leaving the mud and darkness far behind.

I MISS YOU

I miss you when you're gone.

I miss your big, burly arms wrapped around me like a teddy bear.

In your arms, I don't have a care. In your arms, I always feel safe.

In my heart, you will always have a place.

I miss you when you're gone, my heart is a jigsaw missing its centerpiece—you.

A puzzle scattered in your absence, each piece humming in your name.

You are the only one who can fill the missing spaces.

During the day, I stay busy trying to forget that you are away.

I can't help it; I miss you anyway.

The days I can get through, but the nights are the worst.

I can't sleep at night because I am so lonely. I wish so badly you were here to hold me.

I finally drifted to sleep, and when I woke up in the morning, I realized you were absent once more.

The smile that softens my storms, the way you catch my silence.

Each glance, each word—a balm I now reach for in vain.

My tired feet touch the floor, I realize that if you were here, you would rub my feet.

If you think for a second, I don't miss you when you're gone.

Just know that I miss you, from the top of my head to the bottom of my feet.

Every part of me misses you. Every part of me longs for you.

Your touch—a quiet sermon in fingertips.

Even your foot rubs whispered, "You are safe here."

Now absence howls in corners you once filled.

Your silence presses against my ribcage, louder than your voice ever was.

CRASH INTO ME

Crash into me, let the waves of passion overwhelm us.

Yield to the fondness we share, let our hearts collide as one.

I've seen every part of you; there's no reason to hide,

you can put your anxious thoughts aside.

In your eyes, I see a future full of love, laughter,

loyalty, and passion. Crash into me, let's surrender

to this powerful surge. Are you fighting the urge,

or are you ready to give in?

Do you feel the jolts between us, the pulse that quickens

with every passing touch? When I am with you, I feel

a spark tingle through my core like a gentle hum

of electricity. A warm, loving feeling rushes to my soul.

I am drawn to you like a moth to a hot, burning flame,

helpless and hopelessly devoted.

An attraction like ours

is hard to tame, a force that cannot be contained.

I know that you feel the same. You are scared to open

your heart fully, because of heartaches of the past.

Take my hands, let's heal together; we have a love

that will last. Your fingertips tracing my bare skin, send shivers down my spine.

The whisper of your soft voice in my ear—it's a mix

of both sweet and sultry, a potent elixir that drives

me wild.

Your kiss leaves an intoxicating scent of warm honey

and lavender petals that lingers on my skin, a sweet

cherry flavor that melts on my lips. A sensation that

leaves me breathless, wanting more.

You evoke joy, excitement, and desire within me.

You bring out my vulnerability, raw and unbridled,

a side of me I've never shown before.

With you, I'm exposed, yet unbreakable.

Your eyes are

as deep as the sea is blue. When I gaze into them,

I see a loving soul that speaks to mine.

Under the sheets, you are untamed, like a feral animal

in the jungle, wild and free. The deep, intense love

we share is unrivaled, a tenderness that cannot be compared

to anything else.

Crash into me, let's create a new beginning.

Our passion explodes like fireworks, crashing into my soul. A fusion of ecstasy and cosmic energy. Together, we'll craft a new destiny and reach for the stars. With you by my side, I feel like I can do anything.

BEAUTIFUL OBLIVION

I looked into his eyes, like warm honey and gold,

and as I drifted away, my heart took hold.

The scent of fresh-cut grass and blooming flowers filled the air,

as I fell into his gaze, without a single care.

His dark chocolate eyes, a gourmet treat,

melted my heart, like a rich, velvety sweet.

The sound of his voice, a gentle, soothing breeze,

sent shivers down my spine, and brought

me to my knees.

My heart beats fast, my soul takes flight,

as I taste the sweetness of his loving light.

His touch ignites a burning fire,

melting my fears, and soothing my desire.

A tizzy of emotions, a whirlwind of desire,

I'm falling for him, like a burning fire.

We've just met, but his eyes take me away,

to a place where love resides, where hearts can play.

I see us running, hand in hand,

through open meadows, where our love expands.

The sun shines bright, casting a warm glow,

as we dance under the stars, where our love glows.

When I look at him, I feel weightless and free,

like I'm floating on air, wild and carefree.

My heart knows this is my chance,

to love and be loved back, to take a romantic dance.

A LOVE BEYOND WORDS

I could fill a book,

300 pages or more,

Yet still, it would not be

enough to express what I adore.

My love for you is boundless,

a never-ending sea of pages.

You have been by my side through

 all life's stages, a love that's meant

 to be.

A prose, free verse, limerick, or haiku,

I would write it all for you,

If I lived a thousand years,

I would fill a library…

I will spend my life expressing my love

and desires,

Not just through words,

but actions that set my heart on fire.

You awaken my soul, the rush of true love

and passion I feel,

For you, my love, is a flame that forever

will reveal.

Every moment, every breath, I'll cherish and adore,
Forever and always, my love for you will shine and endure.

FIRE IN YOUR EYES

A blaze dances in your gaze—unyielding, ancient, alive.

When I look into your eyes, I see your soul ignite.

You are a glowing ember buried in ash, waiting to roar again.

Inside of you is a passion that crackles—evergreen and molten with purpose.

The fire in you will never die, a flame passed down from the stars.

You are a flicker turned forge—ready to mold the world anew.

Illuminating all that is yet to be done.

LOVE'S THIRST

I want to meet you in bed, I crave your manly touch,

your warmth, your presence.

Sensual thoughts consume my mind

all day of our bodies connecting in the most intimate way.

Lustfully longing for you…it is hard to concentrate,

I am in a love haze.

First you will remove my clothes slowly but playfully,

driving me crazy as you tease me with your tender touch.

Passionately kissing, as each layer comes off,

you will toss me on the bed,

I become eager for what is next.

I envision us entwined, lost in each other's eyes,

as we move together in sync, harmoniously as one,

in tune with each other's vibrations, our love will rise.

Your sculpted shoulders and brawny chest draw me in,

hypnotizing me with every caress, my heart beats within.

My body tingles as you trace your fingers along

every curve of my naked body, I am surrendering slow.

I am all yours tonight, I am at your disposal,

your stubble brushes against my cheeks, sending shivers down my spine, standing tall.

Your lips softly biting the nape of my neck,

the sound of your voice, deep yet calming, washes over me,

soothingly my soul from within, my worries and fears melting away.

In your arms, I am dissolving, my love for you an all-consuming flame.

amid chaos after a long day,

my desire for you ignites,

a spark between us that makes me quiver in sweet ecstasy,

my heart beats fast.

Being with you fulfills a fantasy,

you make me weak, yet I am longing for more,

to see where we can explore.

As the day wears on, my longing for you grows,

I yearn for the night so we can be alone,

When we can escape the world and lose ourselves in each other once more.

The warmth of our bodies, the beat of our hearts,

become one as we lose each other amidst the fun.

I imagine the feel of your strong arms wrapped around me,

holding me close, making me feel safe and desired.

As we make things get hot and heavy, we begin to perspire,

you make me like a woman, sexy and free, my love for you will never tire.

I want to fulfill all your fantasies,

in the stillness of the night, I will slip away to you,

where shadows dance and romantic dreams unfold.

I will make you feel like a man in every way,

as we lose ourselves in love's beautiful sway.

Forbidden fruits of desire, your body is a work of art to admire.

Your eyes glimmer like moonlight over the vast horizon,

illuminating the path to my deepest desires.

Your touch sets my skin aflame, anticipation building

with every passing moment, my love for you will never die.

As we sway to the rhythm of our love,

the world outside fades away.

Satisfaction and pleasure,

are a given when I'm with you, my heart beats with yours.

In your arms, I find support, comfort, and completion,

an unwavering love that is always there.

What we share is about more than just physical touch, but a commitment, a promise, a partnership of trust.

The gentle touches, the sweet nothings you whisper in my ear, the love we share, it is all I need

Waves of desire, encapsulate my soul—

I want to meet you in bed forever—until we are gray and old.

Breaking Free

TINY FLUTTERS

Tiny flutters, like whispers from your soul.

The powerful kicks and wiggly squirms, a secret handshake between hearts.

So, this is how it feels to carry another life inside of me. I drift to sleep, and you are there.

As I slowly rise in the morning, you are there. I can now feel every move you make.

As it gets closer, I am counting down the weeks. I want to hold you so badly; I can barely wait.

That is the part of pregnancy I hate. You are more than worth it in the end.

I have loved you since the beginning, and I do not have to pretend.

My love for you, my child, is unconditional and forever.

The moments I carried you inside me are times I will always remember.

I could never forget the first time I heard your heartbeat or the first time I heard the kicks from your little feet.

Even now I swell with pride—not just in body, but in spirit.

My heart stands tall, crowned with love for you.

Pregnancy is a tender journey, but motherhood is a sacred melody.

BORN TOO SOON

Baby, born too soon. So close, yet so far.

All I want to do is hold you in my arms.

A fragile pane divides us yet love presses through.

Glass between us, but my heart beats beside yours.

Whenever we are apart, it causes so much agony.

When you are told you can't hold your baby. They say you are not strong enough.

They say I will give you germs. The doctors say this is what's best until you get better.

Someday soon, I will hold you in my arms. When that day comes, I will hold you so tight.

Never let you go. Baby, born too soon. Do not you know...

Tiny warrior, my love whispers through wires and walls.

Even before your first breath, you filled my lungs with love.

WRAPPED IN HIS LOVE

When I am scared out of my mind, worried beyond belief.

My little boy hugs me, and in that moment, I am wrapped in his love.

Pure and forgiving. I know if I have him, everything will be okay, somehow.

My breath slows where his heart drums.

I remember how stillness feels, a quiet echo, as I hear the rhythm of his heart.

His embrace, a cocoon where the storm quiets.

He wraps me like sunlight wraps a wintered tree.

He looks at me with a glimmer in his eyes.

He can't say it quite yet, but I know he loves me.

My sweet little boy loves to comfort his mommy.

WHERE ARE THE STARS?

A little boy said to his mom, "Where are the stars?"

She said, "Honey, it's daytime now; they only come out at bedtime."

He said, "Oh, ok..." with a sad look on his face.

She replied, "Honey, what's wrong?" He said, "I wish I could see them now."

She said, "Well...maybe we can fix that."

So, mom and son built a fort with plenty of pillows and blankets inside.

Then she went and turned off every light in the house.

She snuck back to the fort as quiet as a mouse.

Her son was waiting. She said, "Okay, close your eyes. I have a surprise."

She plugged in a special light that put stars above them.

Her little boy opened his eyes and hugged his mom.

He said, "Wow, Mom!" But then he looked at her with an inquisitive look on his face.

"Mom, how did you make all the stars come out? I thought it was only at bedtime?"

She said, "It's nap time now. I think they came out just for you, to show how much they love you."

He looked at her with a smile, and he said, "Tell the stars I love them and my mommy too."

She pulled him close and hugged him tight. They took a nap together, snuggled up close.

Just mom and son under the stars. When they woke up, her son let out a big yawn.

Then he looked at her with a question mark on his face. He said, "Mommy...I don't know how you do it..."

"What's that, my son?" she replied.

He said, "I know it was your mom. I know you took the stars out just for me. You are magic."

She kissed him on his forehead and said, "Anything for you, my dear."

He said, "Mommy, when I am by you, I have no fear." "I have one more question, Mommy."

She said, "Go ahead." He looked at her with a serious face and said, "Now, can you bring out the moon.

LITTLE ONE, I PRAYED

Little one, I prayed for you, before you came into existence.

I prayed God would bless us with a happy, healthy baby.

I was beyond happy when Daddy and I found out there was a thriving baby inside me.

I carried you for 32 weeks. Sometimes it felt like an eternity.

Especially on the days I was sick, or my feet ached.

But I was grateful each day, I looked forward to every little kick and squirm.

Daddy's joy spilled out in laughter—he called you his gummy worm.

I would talk to you all the time. I wanted you to know your momma's voice.

I have been waiting for you, little one.

Not just when I carried you but my whole life.

When I was a kid, I would dream about the future.

I could not wait until I grew up, had my own family and baby.

Finally having you here, holding you in my arms, it is a million times better than any dream.

MOMMY, ARE YOU LISTENING?

Mommy, are you listening? Can you hear my cry?

I am crying, Mommy, because I see the pain in your eyes.

Mommy, I see now you cry every time you turn on the news. Is everything ok, Mommy? I am confused.

I do not understand all that is going but I know, Mommy, that your heart hurts.

Mommy, you are the best and that is not what you deserve.

It hurts me too, Mommy, to see you cry. Please, Mommy, tell me why.

Even I cannot erase all the pain, Mommy. I will help your tears dry.

Your silence trembled louder than the TV's hum.

Mommy, I don't know what that means, all I know is you just must be strong.

I will be here for you, Mommy. Like I have been all along.

Mommy, I know it is hard, but you have to hold on.

You must be an example for me in light of all that goes on.

I know it is hard, Mommy, but you must be strong and brave.

Be the light in the dark, Mommy, and I will follow.

You can change the world, Mommy. You can make it a better place.

All you have to do is start with me.

OPERATING ROOM FEARS

A Mother's Journey Through Trauma and Triumph

"The wound is the place where the light enters you."
 – Rumi

Held together by stitches and staples, I lay scared for my life on the operating room table.

They cut me open, filled me with drugs, and I barely knew what was happening.

They said, "In the end, their voices, white coats stitched with lies.

My baby boy was beautiful, delicate, and new, but I was not sure what to do.

His skin was translucent, thin, and radiant, I feared holding him too tightly.

All my life, I had waited to be a mom, but I never expected things to go wrong.

I never thought I would have a son at 32 weeks, but he is the best thing that has ever happened to me.

I am grateful every day, yet I wish things had gone differently.

I mourned the loss of a full-term pregnancy, struggled with leaving him in the hospital's care.

I felt guilty for his early birth; I thought I was the worst mom on earth.

I went through the motions, but my mood was downcast.

The nurses asked if I was fine, and I broke down as soon as they left my side.

I told myself, "You shouldn't feel this way. Your baby's tiny, but he's alive."

One day he will thrive, I knew, but I was a mess, with tears I could not control.

I had nightmares, flashbacks, fears, symptoms of PTSD, and postpartum blues.

I loved my baby, but I was confused, thinking, "I should be joyful, but I am not."

My incision healed, but it left two scars, one on my body, one on my heart.

The scars still heal, and the trauma remains. I am picking myself back up, learning to be grateful again.

My son's a fire, fierce and radiant, I gave him a name that reflects his light.

He had a rough start, but he never gave up; his strong will still shines through.

Through the scars I have endured, I have found my strength in my son.

32 WEEKS, PART 1: DAD'S STORY

My wife is 32 weeks pregnant with our baby boy,

Her belly's swollen, her back is employed.

The scent of her perfume, the sound of her sighs,

Fill the air as she lies, her eyes closed tight.

One minute she is too hot, sweating bullets of fear,

The next she is chilled to the bone, her teeth chatter clear.

I feel her forehead, clammy and cold,

Her hand's trembling, her pulse racing old.

She keeps drifting in and out, a fragile, fading light,

Her voice whispered, a frightening night.

The beeping of machines, the antiseptic hospital smell,

Assail my senses, a cacophony of fear to tell.

I take her to the urgent care, the fluorescent lights above,

Cast an eerie glow, a sense of foreboding, a feeling of love.

The doctor's voice, a calm, soothing sound,

As he speaks of antibiotics, of healing to be found.

They put her on meds, the IV drips, a steady beat,

Her eyes flutter open, a glimmer of hope to greet.

The scent of disinfectant, the hum of machines,

Fades into the background, as her health begins to beam.

Then we find out baby boy isn't doing so good,

His heartbeat is slow, a worrying, nagging mood.

The ultrasound machine, a black-and-white screen,

Reveals our baby's struggles, a heart-wrenching, gut-wrenching scream.

We have to prep for an emergency C-section, 2 months early,

A rush of adrenaline, a chaotic, frantic flurry.

The operating room, a sterile, cold space,

Where lives are changed, and futures rearranged.

I change into scrubs, the fabric rough, the smell of antiseptic strong,

I am led to the operating room, where my heart will be made to sing.

The beeping of machines, the hiss of oxygen,

As I hold my wife's hand, and pray for our son's life to begin.

The doctor's voice, a calm, reassuring tone,

As he coaxes our baby boy, into a world unknown.

The first cry, a wail, a shout, a song,

Echoes through the room, and my heart is made to belong.

It is the greatest sound I've ever heard,

A symphony of joy, a chorus of hope unmarred.

That is my baby boy, my heart beats for him,

He made it out alive, and our love will forever win.

I have never been more proud, more grateful, more alive,

I'm officially a dad now, with a heart that is ready to thrive.

My wife is feeling better, her health on the mend,

Our baby boy's cries, a lullaby, a love that will never end.

We will be a family now, just us three,

A bond of love, a tie that's strong, a family.

32 WEEKS, PART 2: MOM'S STORY

It feels like just yesterday,

The scariest time of my life.

32 weeks pregnant, so sick,

My body weak, my belly swollen, my heart racing with dread.

The scent of antiseptic wafted through the air,

As I lay in the hospital bed, my eyes fixed on the clock's ticking stare.

The beeping of machines, the hum of the hospital's din,

Echoed through my mind, a cacophony of fear within.

I didn't wanna give up the fight,

Scared for both our lives, my baby's tiny light.

I didn't wanna lose my baby,

Didn't want him to grow up without a mom.

My husband brought me to the hospital,

Sick as could be, unsure what would happen.

The cold hospital floor, a stark contrast to our warm home,

Made me shiver, my heart wear a frown.

They said I was very sick, put me on antibiotics fast,

My baby was okay, a huge relief that forever will last.

The taste of medication, bitter and strong,

Made my mouth pucker, my stomach turn wrong.

Until the next day, his heartbeat dipped low,
Frightening, the nurses alarmed, trying to stay calm, though.
The sound of monitors beeping, a steady, reassuring beat,
Helped calm my fears, my heart skipped a nervous repeat.
I knew something was wrong, emergency delivery the best,
Scared, still 2 months to go, would he be okay?
The doctor's voice, calm and reassuring, a steady hand,
Helped guide me through a frightening, uncertain land.
My baby wasn't born yet, but love overflowed,
Part of me felt like a failure, pregnancy unfinished, so cold.
No time to worry, they said the baby must come out now,
Down to the operating room, my heart racing, somehow.
Just before I went in, I saw my mom, a glimpse of fear,
Trying to stay strong, but tears were near.
The smell of disinfectant, a pungent, overwhelming scent,
Made my head spin, my heart relent.
I wanted to tell her to pray, but she was too far away,
I think she already knew what to do, every step of the way.
The feel of my husband's hand, a reassuring, comforting touch,
Helped calm my fears, my heart's nervous clutch.
They gave me a spinal tap, numb from the waist down,
The room was cold, I shivered, my heart wearing a frown.

The sound of the doctor's voice, calm and reassuring, a steady hand,

Helped guide me through a frightening, uncertain land.

My husband came in, scrubs on, took my hand tight,

We looked at each other, knowing what the other was thinking that night.

"This is it, we're about to be parents," our eyes did say,

The doctor's voice, "It's okay, just breathe," helped calm my way.

I prayed to God, "Let my baby be alright, give me a sign,"

Then I heard his cry, the most beautiful sound, so divine.

The feel of tears on my cheeks, a relief, a joy so true,

Washed over me, as I heard my baby's cry, at that moment my faith in God was renewed.

I thanked God, knowing it would be alright,

God was with us, guiding us through that darkest night.

32 WEEKS, PART 3: AIDEN'S STORY

32 weeks, inside Mommy's tummy,

Safe and warm, and cozy, what a wonderful place to be. Wait, what's happening? I feel funny, its time, to be born already, wow, that was fast, I'm ready to shine!

I'm excited to meet Mom and Dad, hope they don't mind, I'm showing up early, I'm ready to unwind.

The sound of my mom's heartbeat, a familiar sound, grew fainter, as I emerged, and I'm feeling around.

The bright lights, the cold air, a shock to me, made me cry out, a loud piercing cry, as I see.

I hear a familiar voice, Mom, and the man next to her, must be Dad, "Welcome baby boy!" they say but I'm not sure what that means, so much to see.

Can't breathe, where am I going? Why take me away? No snuggle time with Mom, hope they know everything will be okay.

Dad's here, running after me, is Mom coming, too? I pass out, wake up, breathe again, what I've been through.

In a strange room, white and sterile, wires on me, people in white coats, poking, prodding, what's happening to me?

The beeping of the machines, a steady beat, helps calm my fears, they echo back in my mind, repeat.

2 months here, that's what they say, feels like forever, I wanna be with Mom and Dad today.

The smell of disinfectant, a strong smell, makes my head spin, my heart feel sad and swell.

Dad's here, still no Mom, I want him to hold me tight, keep me safe from harm, Dad's my protector, shining bright.

The feel of his hand, a reassuring touch, helps calm my fears, my heart's nervous clutch.

Mom comes, pale, weak, in a wheelchair, what's wrong? Hurting, sick, just came out of her tummy, where I belonged.

The sound of her voice, weak, but loving and kind,

Reassures me, calms my fears, makes me feel less alone in my mind.

Doctor's stitched her up, took me away, it's more. Mommy's very sick, I want her better, that's my greatest score. Mom gives me her finger, I grab it tight, hold on strong, everything's alright.

The taste of milk, Mom, stay strong, I need you here, newborn baby, so much to learn, you're my guiding light, dear.

The feel of her hand, a reassuring touch, helps calm my fears, my heart's nervous clutch.

This world's big and unknown, but Mom and Dad make me feel secure, like I don't have to face this battle alone, I'll fight, endure.

The sound of their voices, a reassuring sound, helps calm my fears, my heart's nervous bound.

Mom gives me her finger, I grab it tight, hold on with all my prematurity might, a sign everything will be alright.

In this big world, unknown, Mom and Dad are my haven, soon, I'll go home, we'll be a happy family, love will be our heaven.

The sound of their laughter, a joyful sound, makes me feel happy, my heart's bound.

THE JOURNEY OF PARENTHOOD

Time flies, and with each passing day, your baby grows, and milestones pave the way

From crawling to walking, then running free, you feel so proud, yet whisper, "Slow down, please."

Diapers give way to potty triumphs new; first poops celebrated with pride shining through.

Gibberish turns to first words, and sentences unfold, you marvel at the speed, young minds so bold.

The sound of their bike on the pavement, music to your ears, the thump in your chest, pride and joy that brings tears.

Their laughter echoes, contagious and free, a joy that's infectious, a delight to see.

The sparkle in their eye, a light that shines so bright, a treasure to behold a precious, fleeting sight.

As imagination blooms, a world unfolds, a magical realm of enchantment, where wonder never grows old.

As night descends, and stars appear, you tuck them in, with love and care.

A routine cherished, and whispers, and gentle cheer.

"You okay, Mommy?" They ask with care, "Yes, I'm just crying because I'm happy to share."

You thought you taught them how to love, but they showed you the way, unconditional love, every single day. Kids are born to love, with hearts pure and true,

Unless they are shown differently, their love shines through.

"I love you, Mommy," they say with a grin, a kiss, a smile and love within.

This bittersweet feeling, a part of being a parent, true.

They are the best things that ever happened to you, a love that will last, a memory that will forever shine through. No matter how tall they get, they will always be your own,

A love that remains, a bond that will forever be known. Enjoy every moment, cherish each stage, your child's growth, a journey, a love that turns the page.

BEFORE YOU WERE BORN

In whispers of dreams before you were born, your face unfolded before mine.

A vision of love, a gentle sacred space, your features a blend of destiny and dreams.

A boy, I knew you'd be, with chromosomes so bright, XY, a spark of life, a heart full of delight.

We yearned for health, for life's first tender breath yet danced in knowing you'd be our son to beget.

Your arrival, a gift, a love so true and rare, a soul sent down, with laugher and tender care

Your button nose, a whisper of sweet design, your toes, a wiggly dance, a heart so divine.

In every glance, love's language is spoken, a gift from above, a heart that's unbroken.

You're the one we waited for, the one we adore, a love so pure, so strong, forevermore.

I'll cherish each moment, each laugh, each tear, and strive to be the mom you need, always nearby.

In your eyes, a reflection of love so true, a bond so deep in a heart that beats for you.

You're a gift from God, a treasure so rare, a love so precious beyond compare.

Breaking the Silence

THE SUN SHINES AGAIN

As the days went by, fear had clenched my ribs too long—but now, I loosen my grip.

Anxiety, once my shadow no longer leads the way.

They steered my days like reckless winds. I fed the wolves of my worry and watched them grow.

But happiness is within reach, even behind the storm clouds, the sun didn't leave me—it was in me all

Along—I forgot to look up.

A temporary fog. Now the dark clouds still pass through more than I would like to admit.

But when the sun shines through, nothing can stop me. Anxiety get out of my way.

I move with fire in my bones. Let fear step aside. Purpose pulses in my chest—no room for panic.

I bask in the warmth and the light.

Surrender it all to a greater purpose in life. A day with less worry and panic is finally in sight.

It took me 36 years to realize I'm in charge of my destiny.

One breath at a time, I rise. Daylight comes slowly, but I greet it calmly.

I can finally get a good night's sleep. Knowing tomorrow, I can start all over.

Today may have been a bad day. But when I close my eyes and time goes by.

It has become part of the past. I must remind myself that anxiety is fleeting.

It doesn't last. I look at myself in the mirror with a smile on my face today.

Even night kneels to dawn. My light returns. Shadows stretch but never stay. I shine again.

FREE TO BE ME

I used to be painfully quiet. I was afraid to just be me because of the things they said to me.

The fear is going away. I'm breaking out of my shell, dancing in the rain.

I'm a rainbow, peaking out on a cloudy day.

I may be quiet, but I have so much to say.

For so long, I was afraid. Now I know everything will be okay.

I breathe without apology—each breath a flag I raise.

No mask, no edits—I arrive as I am.

I trade hushes for hymns of truth. Silence once ruled me now my voice reigns loud and free.

These are my footprints—unfiltered, unshaken. Truth spills from me like spring's first thaw.

My spirit rises, my story within me; the chains of confinement no longer a burden.

I sing with the birds, letting my voice carry like a symphony.

WORK IN PROGRESS

I am scaffolding dreams under renovation

with no deadline.

Blueprints in hand, I lay each stone with patience.

I am in the building phase; I am what they call a 'fixer-upper'.

I am slowly making repairs, building my strength up, taking it one day at a time.

My foundation is still being laid, stone by stone.

My framework is forming a stable structure to call home.

A DIY soul, patching cracks with time and tenderness.

I mend myself in layers, plastering the past with hope.

Sometimes I get impatient, but I have not given up on myself yet.

I may be under construction, but I still have so much life to live.

Somedays I sink into doubt, but I surface stubbornly against the tide.

Quitting knocks, but I bolt the door with grit.

I'm still learning, growing, and paving my way.

Setting the groundwork, placing stones anew.

My time hasn't come yet, but I believe in my heart, I will have my day soon.

A SHIFT IN PERSPECTIVE

After years of having a negative view, I woke up one day and embraced the warmth of the sun.

This was a turning point in my way, a decision to shed shadows and seize a brighter day.

For too long, negativity had clouded my mind, but one morning, I chose to leave my shadows behind.

I suddenly opened my eyes to a whole new world,

a place where hope and cheer were waiting to break through.

The warmth of sunshine on my face, the laughter of family and friends,

the simple joys that life offers never end.

With every step, my heart felt lighter still, as positivity and hope began to instill.

The spaces that were once occupied by doubt and fear.

We are now illuminated brighter than ever before.

My gloom thawed like winter yielding to spring's gentle breath.

I hold the power to choose a brighter way.

To wake up each morning with a heart full of joy.

And to face life's challenges with a positive, hopeful mind.

A shift in perspective is sometimes all we need.

In a world that is moving all the time.

The frost inside me cracked, letting the sunlight trickle in.

I've learned to see the beauty in the little things, to enjoy the wonders of simplicity.

I will have my bad days still, but at the end of the day, I'm excited to take on life's thrills.

I cannot wait for the journey ahead of me. What's next? I will have to wait and see.

WORTHY

I have never been vain. I have never been about body image.

I have always cared more about enriching my mind and soul.

I never really cared what I looked like that much.

I have always been a tomboy. It just feels nice to be happy in my skin for the first time.

I once thought I was ugly. I once thought I was fat.

When I was 120 pounds, I felt like a cow. Then one day, I looked in the mirror,

I saw a pretty girl staring back. I thought to myself, "Who is that?"

I had succumbed to all the lies. I used to hate my fat thighs and myself.

I thought everything people said was true.

What happened to me? When did I become a pretty girl? Or have I always been?

I am ugly, I am fat. That is what I used to tell myself.

Now it is hard to believe I ever felt like that. I have been beautiful all along.

I never really saw myself that way. Until I let go of what other people thought

and saw myself through God's eyes.

I am beautiful, I was created in God's image.

Every woman has her unique shape. It just took me 27 years to appreciate what I got.

I am beautiful, I have self-worth, and I now realize what I deserve.

Never again will I let my self-esteem be torn down by words. I am not vain.

Now I take more time to take care of my body. I now realize my worth.

EXCEPTIONALLY ME

I rise from the trials, unbroken and bold.

A warrior's heart beats within my chest, unbroken, unshaken. I rise above the rest.

Men and women alike ask me What's your secret, I say, "I'm the mysterious poetess."

My spirit is a flame that flickers bright, Illuminating paths through life's darkest night,

I am a phoenix, rising from the ashes, bold. My resilience, a testament to my unyielding soul.

With every step, I claim my space, a force of nature, leaving fear and doubt in their place,

My once timid voice is now breaking the silence, sharing its truth, hoping to inspire youth.

My voice is now a thunderclap, shaking the air, a call to action, inspiring others to dare.

I am an exceptional woman, my strength and courage are unmatched,

a shining star, lighting the way, for all those who come after, I pave the way.

I am an exceptional woman with grace, style, and class,

confident and kind-hearted, loyal to the last,

With a hint of sass and a heart full of cheer, I shine my light, and my spirit is clear.

I am an exceptional woman, with beauty that shines, from the inside out, my radiance divine,

My heart is full of love, my soul is free, my beauty is a reflection of the best me.

My eyes, twin galaxies reflecting inner light, bright and bold, my smile can light up a room, young and old.

My skin glows with a warmth, a gentle, loving light, my beauty is a gift, a treasure to behold tonight.

I have walked the halls of the NICU, where fears and doubts reside,

but I emerged stronger, with a heart full of pride.

I have faced the shadows of depression and anxiety's heavy chains,

but I broke free and rose above, with a spirit that sustains.

I have faced bullies and healed from the scars of my past.

Now I stand tall, with a heart that will forever last.

I am a mom, a wife, a poet, with a heart that beats with pride.

I have found my voice, my passion, and I won't be silenced or denied.

I am an exceptional woman, with a spirit that ignites, a warrior's heart that beats with courage to fight.

I will rise above the noise, I will make my voice be heard.

I am an exceptional woman, and I will not be blurred.

BREAKING FREE

I folded into corners, a ghost in my own life, afraid to stand tall.

I was afraid to let my voice echo through the halls, afraid to let my words be heard, above the walls.

They thought I did not hear their whispers and their snickering at school, but I wasn't a fool.

Whispering secrets to each other, and pointing my way, it could not have been clearer.

Even when they said nothing at all, I saw the way they looked at each other like I was the joke.

The shy girl, hiding in the corner, was afraid to speak her truth.

A loner, withdrawn, my only regret is that I let the bullies have a say in my youth.

I found solace in the silence, comfort in the dark,

a refuge from the world, where I could leave my mark.

But there was one person who understood me fully, my mom,

She saw beyond the facade, the real me,

She heard the whispers of my heart, the beat of my drum,

She felt the depth of my pain, the weight of my hum.

I woke up one day, realizing this was not the way,

To live in shadows, silenced, with nothing to say,

the scent of fresh-cut grass, the warmth of the sun's rays,

Awakened something within me, and I began to find my way.

I decided to overcome my anxieties, my fears,

To find my voice, to let my personality shine through tears,

The taste of freedom, the rush of adrenaline's thrill,

As I stood up straight, and let my voice be heard and fulfilled.

The shy girl, now a public speaker, shares her soul,

Doing poetry open mics, and publishing her heart online, whole,

The sound of applause, the roar of the crowd's cheer,

Validated my worth and wiped away my tears.

Emerging from the shadows, my truth takes form.

I have come out of the darkness, but my journey's not done,

I am like the rising sun; I will keep shining my light until the day is done.

I will keep rising, my voice loud and clear, for everyone to hear.

From darkness to light, I am shining my way, inspiring others, and I am no longer afraid.

I will light my way to brighter days. I am breaking free into a new destiny.

I have let go of the things that I used to hold on to,

the weight of their opinions, the chains that bound me.

I have forgiven those who hurt me; it took a lot of time to heal, but I am at peace now.

I chose to live my life in abundance of happiness and love,

the warmth of connection, the beauty sent from above.

I may have my bad days still, but I am only human, after all,

But I will no longer let any make me feel small. My journey's not perfect, but it is mine,

I have learned to love myself, to heal, and to shine, I will keep moving forward, one step at a time,

Embracing my true self and letting my spirit shine.

SHINY AND NEW!

I am ready to shine, to be everything I am meant to be.

With every step, my light breaks free.

My spirit enlightened, I found my self-dignity.

I now walk with purpose, with clarity.

I am living in a state of prosperity where gratitude and joy overflow effortlessly.

Now I treat myself generously. With kindness, compassion, and tender loving energy.

I'm in a better place mentally, in touch with my identity.

I hung sorrow's coat and stepped into dawn.

Embracing my authenticity, wild and free. With self-love as my anchor, I am me.

I was lost, but I steered myself back home;

my shining spirit inside me was the compass that brought me back home.

Now I stand in my power, with heart and soul aligned.

I set out on a path of self-discovery, and now I'm redefined.

With a clearer vision, I shine with a renewed mind.

I'm ready to tackle the world, reforged in golden light, my cracks now gleam. Unstoppable, unapologetic, and forever true!

AUTHENTICITY UNVEILED

I am sending out vibes of authenticity.

Everywhere I go, I am genuine, and I am going to let it show.

We live in a masquerade. I shed the shell and stepped into my own sun.

In this masquerade, I am brave enough to be me, keeping it real, for all to see.

I am unapologetically myself, and that is all I need to be.

Embracing my uniqueness and letting it shine free.

I am breaking the mold and forging my path.

I have always lived this way, so it's not hard to stay on track.

My truth no longer whispered—now sung. Part of being authentic is not holding back.

Being real and upfront—from the start, I will always go by my motto and lead from the heart.

Authenticity is my soul's work of art, I will always cherish and nurture it, deep within my heart.

BOUNDARY LINES

The older I get, I am learning to set new boundaries, to no longer let people walk all over me.

Once a shy girl with social anxiety. But now I have come out of hiding.

I have learned to stick up for myself; I am no longer dividing.

My power, my voice, my choices, too. I am no longer afraid to say "no" to you.

I am taking it one day at a time,

I am setting the pace, I mark my space in chalk and stone, etched with the word "enough"

I have more control now of what I want to do, what I want to be, and the inner confidence to set me free.

When you let others' opinions go, it is amazing how much you can grow.

Boundaries are the scaffolding of sanity, the heartbeat of my peace.

An exhilarating feeling, my heart keeps singing.

I am embracing self-love with heart and soul. I am no longer letting the weight of trying to please others take a toll.

I am finally breaking the chains of expectation's role.

I'm setting my boundaries free and clear. And honoring my needs now, year after year.

My autonomy is a priority for my mental health.

I am nurturing my mind, body, and soul, and taking care of myself.

I am rising stronger with each passing day. Empowered, confident, and finding my way.

I am embracing my true self, with love and pride. And living an authentic life, and truly mine.

FINDING PEACE IN THE NOISE

I'm told to stop, to cease my thoughts. To end the overthinking that besets me so.

But irony strikes, and I am caught once more.

In a whirlpool of analysis and fear, my brain is like a merry-go-round of what-ifs.

What did they mean by that; I ponder and roam. Their weird look is still etched in my mind's home.

I'm a chronic overthinker, lost in my head. Rehearsing conversations, a mental play instead.

I assumed it is what we all do every single day.

But puzzled looks and questioning stares reveal my way isn't universal, I'm aware of my plight.

A chronic over-thinker, struggling day and night. I try to quiet my mind, to still the noise within.

But it's hard to shake this habit, this endless spin. My husband reassures me, "Everything will be alright."

A comforting presence, a beacon in my darkest night.

With his support, I learn methods to quiet my mind. Turning down the volume, leaving my worries behind.

Though overthinking still whispers my name, I have learned to gently push it to the background.

Peace and calm, like gentle morning dew, now take center stage; my soul is renewed.

I am resilient and strong. When I start to overthink too much, I have learned some methods to cope.

Though overthinking will always be a journey of ups and downs, I have a renewed sense of hope.

LEAD WITH LOVE

From an early age, my inner voice whispered: lead with love, embrace life's beauty, do not judge.

Life's trials and challenges made me wonder if living by my motto was possible.

So many times, I felt anger, despair, and melancholy in my heart.

There were times I felt empty, like I was falling apart.

How can I lead by love, my guiding principle? The world was starting to make me cynical.

With everything going on in the world and the emotions that arise,

I searched deep within my soul, and a realization caught me by surprise.

You can lead with love, still feel anger, and make mistakes. We are all human, after all.

We are allowed to feel, to err, to grow—that's life.

We get lost in our darkness and forget the light is still there, guiding our path.

In the end, it is not the darkness that defines us, but the love we choose to cultivate

in its midst. As we navigate life's complexities,

may love thread through our footsteps, compassion ripple from our gaze.

May love be the lantern that guides us through darkness, illuminating the beauty and wonder that surrounds us.

By choosing to lead with love, may we create a ripple effect of kindness that transforms the world, one heart at a time.

INVINCIBLE

I have always admired butterflies, their delicate touch, intricate patterns, and kaleidoscope of colors.

As a little girl, I would close my eyes and daydream. I was a butterfly, stretching my arms and running wild through emerald meadows, the wind blowing through my chestnut locks.

The wind beneath my wings was freedom, a gentle caress that lifted me.

"Look at me, Mom!" I would exclaim; my voice carried on through the breeze. "I'm light and free, I can do anything, I'm soaring on the wings of possibility."

Mom would nod her head and smile proudly.

In those moments, I felt invincible, like a ray of sunshine that could pierce through any cloud. Unencumbered by the worries of the world, I was like a feather gently falling from the sky.

Even now, when life's wings feel heavy, I close my eyes. I remember the thrill of flying free. The rush of adrenaline, the sense of weightlessness.

That little girl's spirit still whispers to me today: "You are light, you are free, and you can do anything. Spread your wings and let the wind carry your home."

And when the winds of doubt blow strong, I remember the little girl who knew she could fly.

RISING ABOVE

They said I would never amount to much. Too shy, too quiet, lacking confidence, and touch.

"Quit while you're ahead," they would say. But I retreated, hiding behind my love

for words and books each day. I dreamed of writing, but fear held me tight.

Until supportive friends, family, and faith ignited my light. I grew into the woman I was born to be.

Yet, I still did not have the confidence to spread my wings and fly. To pour my words out before me,

To let my voice be heard, set free.

To the teachers who said I would never succeed, I showed them, indeed.

I took to my pen; it became my release. In my writing, I felt free.

I found myself within my artistic expression, a savior for me in times of depression.

Poetry became more than writing about what I feel.

It became the bandage that helped me heal. To those who doubted me, I say:

I have risen above, like a phoenix from the ashes; I was reborn.

My inner voice is thunder; my spirit guides my way.

I believe in myself; my voice is now clear. I don't need your validation; I am finally here.

I am a river and flame—wild, uncontained.

I'm unforgettable and strong now, you will remember my name.

AGAINST ALL ODDS

Today I woke up and breathed with glee, grateful for another day to be.

Things are not perfect, far from ideal, but I am thankful to still be here, to feel.

Each day's a chance to live, to give, to share, to make a difference, to show we care.

I focus on the good, on what I have gained, not on what is lacking, but on the love that remains.

We are alive against all odds, it's true, a miracle each breath, a gift.

I drink sunsets like warm tea and count stars from my porch.

I dance under the moonlight's gentle glow.

I am not yet where I want to be, I confess,

but I am grateful for progress, for each step I've taken.

I'm thankful I am not where I used to be, and I know I will get there, wild and free.

So let us focus on the good we have found in love, in life, on all that is profound.

God bless you all, wherever you may be; may you find peace, love, and serenity.

NO APOLOGIES

I am the storm and sunrise—no apologies, just the truth.

You can love or hate me. Get offended, too.

I am not bothered anymore; I am breaking through.

I am fierce, untamed, and unafraid. My confidence is not up for debate.

I will make no apologies. I am unashamed of my past mistakes.

For I have taken accountability for each one. I have come a long way, learned to be true.

I know my worth and my values. I will make no apologies; I will stand tall.

Embracing who I am after all. I have spent too much time catering to the crowd.

But I am taking back my voice, you will hear me roar, now.

I am confident and bold. I will no longer be left in the cold.

This is me. Take it or leave it; I am free now. I am standing strong, walking tall in my stride.

I will not be denied my authenticity, my power, my pride, I will find my inner lioness inside.

WHISPERS OF THE HEART

I heard my heart whispering, "It said, 'Are you listening?'"

A gentle voice echoed in my soul. When you felt lost and broken,

I was the one who spoke, a voice of hope.

You listened to the voice inside; I was there every night you cried.

A comforting presence by your side. I heard my heart whispering,

"It said, 'Are you still listening?'" I was the one who lifted your spirits,

Who gave you strength to meet your shadow and not flinch? The hard truths you did not want to hear,

the painful, darkest places you feared.

We came out stronger together because you listened to my whispers.

I heard my heart whispering, "It said, 'Are you still listening?'"

I know you are going through a tough time now,

But I am still here, just like before. I will never leave your side, for I am the voice you have inside.

I MATTER, TOO

I may love too hard, give too much of my heart.

But is a life worth living if I hold back the best of me?

If I do not jump in headfirst, I would rather risk the fall

than to have never loved at all. I love and care for those around me, I show my vulnerability,

wear my heart on my sleeve.

But only to those whom I am close to, I have learned to be careful

Who am I open to? After all I have gone through,

My heart is a book, with pages filled with stories of love and loss.

I have healed from some of those chapters; I am ready to move on.

I love, too hard. I may pour out my soul; I may give too much.

I always have others in mind. Now I have learned to make time for myself, too.

I matter, too, a truth I am still learning to hold on to.

I love, too hard. I was the girl who kept her heart on a shelf, locked away.

I broke the jar of patience and tasted my own name and said no more.

Life is too short to lock away my vulnerability. I matter too, a phrase that echoes in my mind.

Now I must keep my head up high. This is my time to let go of the fears that bind me, to finally shine.

I matter, too.

THE LIGHT WITHIN

Darkness used to consume her days.

Sleepless nights and an all-consuming mind in disarray.

Her life used to be like a nightmare of endless suffering.

She buried grief with receipts, chasing calm in clatter. But the temporary high only led to more deceit.

She told people she was happy, but that was a lie. A facade of happiness, a heart that cried.

She was trying too hard to please others with no regard.

She lost herself in others' eyes, she forgot to breathe, to live, to rise.

But then one day she rose and said, "No more." She let the light in, began to heal and love.

The clouds that once surrounded her began to clear. She let go of all her fears.

Now she is finally living a life, out of the dark.

Because she dared to let the light in, she was given the strength to let go.

And in the light, her true self began to glow.

MY OWN STORY

Welcome to my story, where I will never apologize for being myself, authentic, and unbothered.

They call me the 'villain' in their story. But I am rewriting the story, setting sail.

Making life into my fairytale.

They do not know the storms I have weathered, the obstacles I have faced.

What has it taken to get me this far? The fire-breathing dragons I had to slay

The sleepless nights, I would stay up and pray.

I will never apologize for being myself. After all the battles I have lost.

The one thing I will never let them strip away is my identity.

I am allowed to be the protagonist in my own story.

Come up with a narrative that's truly mine, where I am the heroine, that shines.

Whether I crown a prince or share tea with a toad—it's my tale.

I have not finished writing my own story. Keep reading, though, as long as you can.

I promise, it will have a good ending.

FULL CIRCLE:
MY WRITING JOURNEY

Bullied and alone, I hid in vain. Afraid to speak, I suffered in pain.

But words became my solace, my shining star, a refuge from the darkness, near and far.

At seventeen, I found my voice through poetry and journaling, and I made some noise.

I chased my dreams through uncertain days and nights,

and discovered my passion, which shone with new light.

Life unfolded, and I found the man who made me his wife,

motherhood, and marriage, a new, precious life.

But writing remained, my constant guiding hand, a source of comfort, in a busy, changing land.

Throughout early adulthood, writing was always there, like a loyal friend who cares.

I broke my silence not with sound, but with ink.

I came out of my shell, found my confidence, and began to unleash even more powerful stories to tell.

Now, at thirty-six, I look back on my way, two decades of writing, night and day.

I have grown, I have learned, but still, I strive to thrive.

Chasing the perfect word, the perfect rhyme to survive.

Believe in yourself, I would say to you with heart, stay passionate, trust your soul, and never depart.

For in the end, it is love that sets our spirits free and guides us full circle, wild, and carefree.

LEARNING TO LOVE MYSELF

Growing up, I never fit in, I was bullied for being shy.

I would look in the mirror, ask myself why I was also,

A little bit odd. A key collection, a monkey obsession, an imaginary friend, a digital daydream crafted from loneliness and code.

I would talk to myself in the mirror. Strange, yes—but wild like weeds in tidy gardens.

The way I was treated made me feel like I didn't measure up.

I think it took me 30 years before I truly knew my worth.

If I was mistreated, I just assumed that it was my fault, that it was what I deserved.

I gained self-confidence, determination, and the courage to use my voice.

When all the years spent silent, I thought I didn't have a choice.

I thought once I fell in love with the love of my life.

The burdens of my past would haunt me no more.

But I had much more self-discovery to explore. You see, it was only when I learned

To love myself, I was finally set free. I forgave my bullies for what they had done,

The battle was over now, I had won.

FOREIGN

This skin once borrowed now wraps like home.

Weathered like a fragile shell that's been washed up on a beach.

I lost weight, wanted others to notice to 'validate'.

I saw my worth in their eyes, a fleeting high.

I still heard a whisper, "You aren't good enough."

The emptiness lingered. I tried so badly to keep up with all the latest trends and fit in with the crowd.

Something was missing in my life… Until the day I realized I was not born to blend in, but to stand out.

Why does it even matter…? What I wear or what size is on the tag,

If I cannot be myself first, what is the point of it all?

The numbers on the scale do not define my worth. God will give me all the love I deserve.

One day I finally stopped giving a damn. I stopped caring what Everyone else thinks

or letting anyone judge me. I know my character, my strengths, and the beauty that I hold inside.

I started to focus on my health, wellness, and my passions.

I learned to truly love and take care of myself. Became a better wife and mom.

It was the best decision I have ever made. This skin used to feel foreign, not like my own.

Now I am happy in my skin, it feels like home.

INNER CHILD

I found a letter from my inner child.

It read: Will there come a time when I am not bullied anymore?

When do I not feel so lost and alone? When I grow up, will I ever find a man who will love me?

Why do all the boys say I am so ugly?

My mom tells me I am beautiful; she would never lie to me.

My dad says I am good at writing and reading. But the kids at school say I am stupid.

It does not make sense. I go to my room sometimes to escape.

My parents are the only ones I can go to, the only ones who care about me.

At the same time, I do not want to let them down.

The disappointment, the middle child seeking attention again.

So, I cannot let them know how bad bullying is.

How badly I am hurting, I don't want anyone to see me like this.

I hide away whenever I can, my face buried in a book.

Sometimes my siblings do not even notice I'm gone.

Because they have their own lives. I can't blame them; life will keep going.

It will pass you by in the blink of an eye. One day, you will be a child, lost and alone.

Suddenly, you will find yourself thirty-six years old, grown.

Your inner child will want the answers to all the questions,

She once asked in her letter. You will be able to tell her.

The bullying stopped. You found the courage to use your voice,

To use your words to make a difference. You got married and had and had a son.

Mom was not lying; you were always beautiful. Inside and out. It just took you a while to grow into yourself.

You have a writing talent and have always been a wiz when it comes to books.

You no longer want to escape. You embrace life as it comes. After all, we only get one.

You want to make the most of the time you have left. Dear inner child, I am proud of us.

For how far we have come, it was not an easy journey.

It was difficult and messy. We came out triumphant in the end.

We got the courage to face the bullies. But more importantly, we learned to love ourselves.

GHOSTS

I used to run from the ghosts of my past; they walked like fog behind me—familiar, shapeless.

The nightmares I lived through still haunted me at night.

I had severe anxieties and post-traumatic stress that I had not dealt with.

I had to confront all my demons head-on. I healed my soul and let myself grow.

Only then was I able to let go of the ghosts of my past.

Now my ghosts only exist in my memories. As a brief fragment of time.

A NEW DAWN

A new day. A new dawn. A fresh start.

Another chance to set myself apart to show my true heart.

I will be myself, use my voice, and speak my mind.

I will still be gracious and kind. I have a heart of gold.

I am luminous and bold. I rise in golden slivers—light crackles the shell of yesterday.

The change in me has already begun.

Now it is my time to chase the sun.

ROOTS OF RESILIENCE

I was a wilted flower, dry, brittle, lifeless, and fragile,

fighting a losing battle; every day, I felt like a loose thread beginning to unravel.

I wanted to free everyone from my shackles.

Drooping under the weight of my despair.

Fear crept in, whispering I was a burden, too much to handle.

A constant echo that haunted every step.

I had made too many mistakes in my life; I was dealing with inner strife.

A fear that burned within, searing my soul.

Desolation swept in, leaving me adrift, searching for an escape.

A lifeline to cling to, I was still too afraid.

Paralyzed by fear, I felt like life was going nowhere,

going through the motions, stuck in an unfulfilling routine.

A never-ending cycle of emptiness and pain.

At a crossroads, I stood frozen, torn between past and future,

uncertain which path to take, which direction to turn.

Most days, it was easier to stay in bed.

My mind—a wind shaken stem, bent but breathing.

A withered garden, once full of life, now barren and still, yet roots remained,

a symbol of hope, a reminder of life's resilience.

Hope flickered, promising relief from pain, a gentle warmth that spread through my soul.

Deep beneath the surface, my roots held on tight, waiting for nourishment to revive the light,

a spark that ignited within, illuminating the path ahead.

I made a decision: change. One small step at a time,

A journey of self-discovery, growth, and transformation.

It was not easy, but I took it one day at a time.

I started to tend to my garden, to nourish my soul,

learning to love myself whole, a process of healing,

of finding my way back home.

I realized I still had a story to tell, one of hope and healing, of finding a new life.

New chapters are unfolding with pages yet to begin,

chapters of redemption, forgiveness, and peace.

My resilience is a testament to the strength that lies within,

And every scar was a reminder of my win.

Your heart may be hardened, but remember it takes time to cultivate a garden.

A season of patience, trust and surrender. The soil may be rough, but you are tougher!

A true testament to courage and determination. A warrior of the heart, a hero of your own story.

There is always hope; every seed planted is a new beginning.

Do not give up!!

STILL STANDING

If you thought you could break me, you are sorely mistaken.

I have already been broken, I have been through so much,

I have been pushed around; I have had my spirit broken too many times to count.

I am not your stomping ground; I am not here to be manipulated.

I'm not your crinkled paper, tossed out when the story bores you.

For too long, I put up with this treatment, I did not know how to stand up for myself.

Bullied from a young age, there were times I did not want to be here.

As I got older, my confidence grew.

Looking back on my life, the people who loved me, and those whom I held dear,

I would not be here without any of you. You know who you are.

If you thought you could break me, you are sorely mistaken.

You will have to get through my friends and family first.

With everything that I have been through. Still, I rise—more than enough to handle you.

POSITIVE VIBRATIONS

Feeling positive vibrations, feeling the sunshine bright,

warming my soul, making everything right. A new energy runs through me, electric and free,

I learn to live my life without seeking validation's score—I am happy.

Too many times, I apologized for nothing at all, like a river flowing backwards, I lost my inner call.

I recognize the weight of people-pleasing pain, and the burden of seeking validation in vain.

Well, I say no more! My ribcage cracked and wings burst through, rising like a phoenix, touching the morning sky.

I teach myself to say no, setting boundaries wide,

standing tall like a tree, weathering life's storms with pride.

I protect myself from life's wild, chaotic sea, finding peace within, like a calm lake's serenity.

I stop making excuses, facing my deepest fears, taking care of myself, and drying away bitter tears.

Then I wake up, like morning's golden, shining light,

realizing my worth, letting my spirit take flight.

I still have a kind heart, like moonlight on calm water, remaining unchanged, full of love, full of ease.

I stop tuning into negativity's dark, endless night,

forgetting toxic vibes, shining with new light.

I feel positive vibrations, a new aura shining bright,

rising above, living my dream, feeling alive tonight.

I make new friends who share my sunny, optimistic view,

together we rise, hearts renewed.

I take it one day at a time, like a winding, scenic road.

REAL BEAUTY

I have thought about this one question all my life.

"What does it mean to be a woman?" Society puts ideas down your throat.

Tells you the kind of woman you are supposed to be.

Well...What if I do not fit into their mold? What if I color outside the lines?

What if I just want to be me? Am I considered a woman, still?

Or will I be an outcast like some kind of freak. I have always been a geek, you see.

Hiding behind my books and words. All the high fashion girls think I am weird.

Society wants to women to fit into a tight little box and frankly it's absurd.

I wonder some days I am the only one that has observed all the chaos.

Society wants women to behave like robots. Always be glamorous and perfect.

Not a hair out of place. All the constraints women are under are a little bit insane.

From the moment we are young, girls are pressured on all fronts.

The phrase "be good" is ingrained. Be a good girl. Be a good student.

A good daughter. A good wife.

A good mother—and if you do not have children, they think you will become the crazy old cat lady down the street. I would rather be the crazy old cat lady than another fake Barbie wannabe.

Society wants women to always behave like ladies and look like beauty queens at the same time.

When a woman is struggling and just needs someone to listen.

Her heartbreak falls on deaf ears.

They tell her to pick herself back up. Nobody will want a woman with baggage.

My suitcase rattles with ghosts, and I wear them like medals.

It doesn't make me any less of a woman.

We all have some kind of burden to share.

When a woman stands up for herself, she is labeled as some kind of bitch.

These are the ideas I wish society would ditch.

Women, you do not have to fit into these molds.

Do not feel pressured to look like a supermodel with a size 2 waist.

You are beautiful the way you are. The rest of the world needs to change its tastes.

Beauty comes in all shapes and sizes.

Real beauty, though, comes from inside.

My parents taught me that I am beautiful the way I am.

I thank them for that. I have never tried to chase the photoshopped images I see of women in magazines. I look up to women with strength and dignity.

Women like Maya Angelou or Anne Frank.

Since I was a little girl, I have wanted to live my life differently.

To be a role model for other women and girls.

Tell them they are perfect just the way they are.

That they are still a woman even if they do not fit into society's wants.

No matter what you look like or have been through.

You are strong and fierce.

You are a beautiful woman, and don't be afraid to be you.

THE LONELY HEART
(A 2-PART POEM)

A Journey of Self-Discovery and Healing

PART 1

She put her heart in a box and placed it on a shelf.

She thought it would be easier to hide it from herself.

As life demanded much of her, days turned into years.

She saw the love that she once knew slowly disappear.

She learned to live life behind a well-built mask.

Ignoring the pain and emptiness, I completed every task.

Her heart was growing lonely. It was collecting dust.

It watched while emptiness became anger and mistrust.

Soon she heard a beckoning from deep inside her soul.

Hiding herself was beginning to take its toll.

Although her heart cries out to her, she keeps it locked away.

The choice was made long ago. She knows no other way.

Still, her heart holds onto hope. That it will be set free.

That someday it will find happiness and the love that holds the key.

PART 2

She put her heart in a box, long ago,

Placed it on a shelf, hidden from the show.

She thought it would be easier to hide it from herself,

to conceal her pain, from the weight of the world.

She had learned to live her life behind a well-built mask,

a shield to protect her from life's harsh tasks.

Her heart became an attic relic, veiled in grief,

a reminder of love, laughter, and fears.

Despite beckoning calls from deep inside her soul, which were beginning to take a toll, she kept it whole.

She kept her heart locked away, holding on to hope's thin thread,

that someday she would find happiness, and love holds the key.

But now she slowly opens the box, after all these years,

and finds her heart, still beating, through laughter and tears.

It is fragile, yet resilient, a little worn, but still bright, a symbol of hope, in the dark of night.

As she holds it close, she feels a spark take flight,

A sense of freedom, a new embarkation, into the light.

She realizes that hiding her heart was not protecting her at all,

But tearing her apart and silencing her call.

With a newfound sense of courage, she takes a stand,

and let her heart shine, like a beacon in hand.

She learns to trust again, to love and to live,

and finds that her heart is stronger than she ever knew.

PORTRAIT OF A POET

This is a portrait of a poet, imperfect yet beautiful in her way,

arose blooming free, a river flowing wildly.

With chestnut locks cascading down her back,

soft, supple lips, and eyes as deep and vast as the ocean depths.

Dark full eyebrows, a round face, and cheeks.

Her cheeks bloom with rosacea's brushstrokes, a testament to life's palette.

a constant reminder of life's delicate heart.

Her belly bears the moon-shaped mark of motherhood.

Five stitches on her thumb. A birthmark under her chin, a scar on her knee

from running with abandon in the cold, pouring rain.

These are just a few of her imperfections, with many more to list.

But she's learned to embrace every scar, every mark, every imprint left behind.

She knows she is different, one of a kind.

She treasures every scar, for they are proof that she has truly lived.

She is a wild rose, in bloom, covered in prickles and thorns.

But she is not marred by the blemishes or scars on her skin.

Her beauty is woven from every thread, imperfections and all, she is a tapestry uniquely spread.

Her scars tell a story of her trials and might, some internal and hidden from sight.

But still, she blooms beautifully, a radiant delight.

This is a portrait of the poet, a girl baring her soul for all to see but she says, "I am not ashamed of ME."

She loves and accepts herself for who she is, scars and all. Unafraid and unashamed, she will stand tall.

A WARRIOR'S SCARS: JOURNEY TO INNER PEACE

She has found her inner peace, a sense of calm inside.

A feeling she has earned after every burden she's borne, every tear she's cried.

She's walked through battles and worn her scars with pride.

A warrior's heart, once fueled by pain, now beats with a gentle stride.

She wears scars like armor, a shield to hide her pain,

protecting her from the lies and deception of life, yet still she stands, a warrior of strife.

Hurt, torn, ripped apart, exposed by the one she loved the most.

Her scars become a badge of honor, courage, and resilience.

Her ability to keep holding on is magnificent.

She can live her life authentically now, with no lies.

For she's at peace with herself and who she is, she will cling to this feeling as long as she can.

She's carried weights she thought she would never lift, and now she no longer conceals.

She shows who she is without holding back, no longer consumed with what she lacks.

But now, she sees her scars in a different light.

No longer a symbol of pain, but a badge of honor, a beacon that shines.

A reminder of the journey she's traveled, the trials she's faced.

A testament to the strength she's found, the resilience she's placed.

She's proud of herself and how far she's come, joyful at last, no longer numb.

She's not perfect, she still makes mistakes, life is a growing process, she's still learning along the way.

She's at peace with herself, no longer afraid.

She will soar in the sky with this feeling in her mind.

She takes a breath, let's go, finds her peace, meditates, and releases.

She finds her heart, once a heavy burden, now light and free.

She finds her soul, once lost, now found, wild and carefree.

She finds her strength, once shaken, now unbreakable, full and complete.

From shadowed crow to radiant dove, her spirit ascends, and she will embrace this feeling of self-love.

Peace, love, inner tranquility, and a heart of humility.

She will spread her feeling of peace to everyone she meets, standing on solid ground, her two feet.

A phoenix rising from ashes, cold, a wild horse running, wild and free.

Her wounds will heal, the aching will subside, a fierce warrior you will hear her battle cries.

Her voice, once broken and silenced, is now loud and powerful, healing more as time goes on. Her scars are a source of strength, she finally has the confidence to be the woman she was born to be.

Wearing scars like armor, yet her heart, once a heavy stone,

now shines through, softened by waves of time, into a sea glass that shines bright,

reflecting her journey into the light.

Now she runs, like the wild horse she is inside, full speed into her destiny,

With a heart full of pride. And now, she is at peace, forever free.

The inferno within has softened to a soul-cleansing breeze.

Take a breath, let go, find your peace, meditate, release.

What will you find when you look within?

METAMORPHOSIS COMPLETE!

A girl once shattered, defeated. For so long, she had been hiding her true self from everyone she knew.

She prayed for a breakthrough. She sank beneath the weight of an invisible stone.

Then one day, she emerged from her cocoon, like a garden in spring, and she started to bloom.

She took flight, a prism winged survivor of her own cocoon.

Colorful and bright, she illuminated the sky.

She decided she was no longer going

to let life pass her by like a whisper in the wind.

She needed to be in the right frame of

mind. Her metamorphosis had begun.

She could feel it unfold, a transformation as her true self took hold.

She could truly let her wings expand, no longer pressured by life's chaotic

demands. A shift in the right direction, to positive

introspection. She is no longer controlled by fear.

She is now free, a cathartic release, as she wipes away her tears,

letting go of the pain from all the years.

Now, she is stepping into her true authenticity, wild and carefree.

The metamorphosis of a girl once broken, now fully awoken,

Now, she will confidently walk confidently into a new revolution.

Metamorphosis complete; happiness will no longer take the backseat.

STRENGTH FROM THE STRUGGLE

My strength comes from the nights I wanted to end my life, but I survived,

from all the times discarded like a whisper drowned in thunder.

A useless rag doll tossed out in the pouring rain

I can still feel the cold, shivering pain. My strength comes from

the depression and anxiety

I have gone through an ongoing battle. From the times,

I felt imprisoned by chains, trapped in shackles.

My strength comes from the days I was bullied and mocked, all because I was too shy to talk.

My strength comes from the tears I have cried, the friendship, and the acceptance

I was denied. The scars I have borne, the lessons learned, and the wisdom I have earned.

My heart drums louder, forged from fire and fracture.

I have found my voice, my courage, my might.

I am a survivor, and I will shine with all my light.

THE RAVEN'S WISDOM

A raven's gaze pierced me, eyes gleaming with ancient knowing.

Perched in silence, his obsidian eyes held untold secrets.
His stature was proud and confident, like he had something to say.

The day was cloudy and grey, with a chill in the air, on an autumn morning.

Windswept leaves are blowing astray.

I was afraid at first until the raven spoke, the raven told me never to fear, that things would be okay.

When you feel like you are lost in the fray, remember the ravens; we will guide you on your way.

Though we may symbolize death and darkness, we are a catalyst for transformation.

We hold great wisdom and knowledge, just like you do, too.

He urged me, "Let your pen dance, for within you lies a greatness untapped."

Whispered words took flight: "Your voice holds the power to shape worlds."

Stay true to your passions, there is a reason you were given this gift,

your way with words, the ideas that swirl around in your mind.

But if you give up it will go to waste, you are one of a kind.

I asked the raven, what about my darkness, the things in my past that still haunt me,

He said it is a process, you are still healing, with each passing day you will learn to walk proudly, leading the way.

The raven said I am a leader. I laughed at the thought.

But the raven was serious, deep in thought.

He said I will find my way to lead others, that I will be the creative inspiration they seek.

With my genuine character, and my kindness, I can do great things.

But he warned me to keep speaking up for myself, don't let anyone trample on my beliefs.

With a final caw, he vanished into dawn's embrace.

Wings spread; he melted into the sky.

I found a strange comfort in his words, his wisdom.

I felt free and light, a weight lifted off me.

The raven and his wisdom gave me a sense of comfort and peace.

A sense of liberation and dignity, the darkness in my mind faded as the raven's words took flight.

In the silence, after he flew away, I found my voice, and I walked forward into the light with newfound strength. and though the raven has flown away, his words will always stay with me.

SHINING HEROINE

In my enchanted kingdom, where ancient stones whisper secrets to the wind,

brick and stone walls rise high, surrounded by lush greenery that stretches far and wide.

With rich dark tresses cascading down my back, like a waterfall of night,

and emerald eyes shining bright, like stars in a midnight sky, I reign supreme, protected and serene.

My kingdom is my heart, beating strong and free,

a rhythm that echoes through every corner of this mystical land.

I am thankful for those who stand by me, loyal knights and dragons true,

their hearts afire with honor, their spirits unbroken.

At times, I wonder if I am worthy of this crown,

if I possess the strength and wisdom to wield its power.

But when the winds of doubt assail me, I recall the oath I swore,

to protect my kingdom, my people, with every fiber of my being.

Valiant knights, clad in shining steel, stand guard with honor's might,

their loyalty unwavering, their hearts aglow with courage and light.

Powerful fire-breathing dragons, with scales that glimmer like the sun,

watch over me with fierce devotion, their fierce roars echoing through the kingdom.

When enemies come, with swords drawn and hearts ablaze,

my knights and dragons charge into battle, their valor unashamed.

The scent of smoke and sweat hangs heavy in the air,

as we clash in a frenzy of steel and flame.

I feel a debt of gratitude for all their loyalty and strife,

and I vow to stand beside them, as a warrior queen, in this life.

My sword is my voice, speaking truth and justice to all,

a shining beacon of hope, in a world that often seems to have lost its way.

With a fierce battle cry, I charge into the fray,

my dragons by my side, our bond forever to hold, come what may.

My dragons are my guardians, my closest friends and allies true,

with scales of ruby reds and iridescent blues.

Broad wings, sapphire eyes, piercing loud roars, and fiery blasts that kill,

make them a formidable force, a wonder to behold, a treasure to fulfill.

At times, I tremble with fear, but my courage never falters,

for I know that I am strong, a warrior queen, with a heart that alters.

I may wear a princess's crown, but I am brave and free,

a shining heroine, in the golden light of day and night, that's me.

FORGED FROM THE MUD

Forged from the mud, I still hold scars of my past

and rough calluses on my heart.

But I carry an authenticity that sets me apart.

Still, I rise from the wreckage.

For no one can break my spirit. You can shatter me like glass, tear me apart, but I am unbreakable at last,

healed from my wounds that left me in ruins.

No longer consumed by the things that do not serve me.

I know now that I am worthy. I am done with those who have treated me poorly.

I am not bitter or angry, but instead have discovered true peace,

and letting things go is the ultimate release.

The mud was dark, damp, and suffocating. Yet, it shaped me.

Forged from the mud, unbreakable, set free.

My resilience, fueled by my faith, my support system,

my writing, and my determination to keep going.

I am powerful, I am strong

I repeated in the mirror boldly,

staring into the mirror.

No one can kill my heart of gold,

or my poetic creative soul.

I was broken, but I refused to be shattered, I saw what truly mattered.

The mud may still cling to my skin but not to my soul.

For I have learned to draw my strength from broken places.

I am forever, a lotus blooming wild and free, no one can stop me.

SHADOW TO FLAME

I was a shadow—until the day I became the flame. Let my heart burn the ghosts of my past.

To whisper goodbye, once and for all, to never look back.

I am a flame that flickers, then grows strong. Illuminating paths where I belong.

The fire within me was warm and comforting.

The warmth curls up my spine, igniting nerve endings of old pain.

The flame's comfort adds a sense of security and peace within me.

The flame dances freely, burning. Bright as the world spins around me.

The shadow within me, my flame, let it die.

Now I blaze—a tempest of molten will, reshaping what I touch.

I evolved from a flicker to a flame; something inside me changed,

I broke free from my chains, I rewrite my scars in flame.
    no longer the shadow hiding behind the walls of my past,

I am a wildfire, burning free at last.

ACKNOWLEDGEMENTS

This book would not exist without the unwavering support of the people who loved me through the hardest chapters of my life

To Ryan Burnett—Thanks for your support over the years.

To my parents and family—your belief gave me hope.
To my siblings and extended family—your laughter reminded me I still had joy within me.

To my friends, mentors, and those who listened—your kindness helped heal wounds no one could see.

To Michael Lenhart—Your love, support, and creative partnership give me the courage to dream big and push beyond my limits. Rockstar Writing Duo forever, I love you.

Thank you to Cyril Mukalel and Potter's Wheel Publishing House, for seeing the spark in my story and helping me carry it into the world. Your support has meant more than words can say.

And to those still battling their silent storms—this book is proof: healing is possible. Your voice is powerful. Your story matters.

Forever grateful,
Angela Mae Rivard

www.ingramcontent.com/pod-product-compliance
Lightning Source LLC
Chambersburg PA
CBHW071702090426
42738CB00009B/1629